The Palestine Question

Raymond Carroll

FRANKLIN WATTS
NEW YORK | LONDON
TORONTO | SYDNEY | 1983
AN IMPACT BOOK

Map courtesy of Vantage Art, Inc.

Library of Congress Cataloging in Publication Data

Carroll, Raymond.
The Palestine question.

(An Impact book)
Bibliography: p.
Includes index.
Summary: Discusses the complex problem of the land
known historically as Palestine including to which,
if any, people it belongs, and the possibilities of
a peaceful settlement of the question.
1. Jewish-Arab relations.   [1. Jewish-Arab relations.
2. Palestine—History]   I. Title.
DS119.7.C356 1983   956   82-20086
ISBN 0-531-04549-8

WI

Contents

The
Palestine
Question

1

The Intractable Question

Open hostilities began on May 15, 1948. On that day, less than twenty-four hours after the establishment of Israel, the Arab armies of Egypt, Jordan, Iraq, Syria, and Lebanon invaded the fledgling Jewish state. The objective was to "drive the Israelis into the sea" and assure Arab domination of the land known historically as Palestine. Unexpectedly, the greatly outnumbered Israelis not only repelled the attacks but threatened to invade the invaders. Stunned by Israel's military successes, the Arab countries sued for peace.

The struggle for Palestine, however, was far from over. Since the "War of Independence," as the Israelis call the fighting in 1948 and early 1949, three additional full-scale wars and countless acts of violence have erupted. And the end is not in sight. Today, four million Palestinian Arabs, either exiled in neighboring Arab countries or living unhappily under Israeli rule, make no secret of their hunger for revenge.

It is a complex problem. To the Israelis, the Palestine question is a matter of their survival as a Jewish state in the land of their biblical ancestors. To the Palestinian Arabs, who inhabited the land for over a thousand years and who formed ninety percent of the population at the beginning of this century, it is a struggle to regain a country from which they have been unjustly dispossessed. To much of the rest of the world, the Palestine issue is one of those intractable questions in which neither side has a monopoly on logic or virtue.

A STRIP OF LAND

Sometimes it is difficult for outsiders to understand what the hate-filled dispute is all about. Looking down from a jet plane or glancing through an atlas, Palestine appears to be just another arid and inhospitable land. Its limits have never been precisely defined, but in modern times the country has been generally considered as bounded by the Mediterranean on the west, the Egyptian Sinai peninsula on the south and southwest, the kingdom of Jordan on the east, and Syria and Lebanon to the north. The state of Israel is now recognized by most countries of the world as the legitimate political authority within much of this territory; it occupies the rest of it as the result of victories in wars with neighboring Arab states.

People have been killing each other over this uninviting strip of land down through the centuries. Canaanites and Hebrews, Babylonians and Greeks, Egyptians and Romans, Crusaders, and Turks—all have spilled their blood in the hills and deserts of Palestine.

Why so much slaughter? One reason is the land's location as a geographical bridge between what used to be called Mesopotamia, with its rich Tigris and Euphrates valleys, and the fertile Nile Valley of Egypt. Palestine*, in short, was a crossroads, through which passed

---

* The name derives from the Philistines, an Aegean Semitic people who inhabited the coastal areas of Palestine in ancient times. Strictly speaking, the country—which has been variously called Canaan, Israel, Judah, and Judea—has been known as Palestine during only two periods. One was between the second Jewish war with Rome (second century A.D.) and the Arab conquest (seventh century A.D.). The second was during the British Mandate (1920–1948). Since Palestine is the most generally accepted name for the region, however, it is used in many contexts in this book.

[2]

an incredible variety of migrating tribes, richly laden caravans, prophets and plunderers, victors and vanquished. As new groups continued to jostle for elbow room in the country, little wonder that conflict—and copious bloodshed—was the result.

Another reason for the violence that has characterized the history of Palestine is religion. The country is unique in its hold on the imagination of Jews, Christians, and Muslims. Indeed, the problems of Palestine have been greatly sharpened by the intensity of religious emotion that the country—and especially the city of Jerusalem—arouses in hundreds of millions of people. Wars have been fought and an enormous number of lives have been given for control of the Jews' Western, or "Wailing," Wall, the Muslims' Dome of the Rock, and the Christians' Church of the Holy Sepulchre.

THE CONFRONTATION

Chiefly, today's Palestine question has to do with Jews and Arabs. Over the centuries, both groups have developed deep historical roots in a place both regard as a Holy Land. Both have strong emotional ties to it. On top of all this, there is the modern problem of nationalism. In the nineteenth century, for a variety of reasons, Jewish and Arab nationalism revived at roughly the same time. It is the confrontation of these two rival nationalisms—each laying claim to the same land—that has produced the Palestine question. It has also produced the Arab-Israeli antagonism that threatens the peace of the Middle East.

The issue of Palestine—to whom does it belong? what should be done about it?—will not be easily ignored. Palestine is one of the world's most dangerous powder kegs. Both Arabs and Jews are bristling with modern armaments. Given the profound animosity between the two sides, the specter of further Arab-Israeli wars will continue to haunt us.

[3]

2

The Promised Land

People have inhabited the land of Palestine for perhaps two hundred thousand years. The earliest inhabitants were Paleolithic (Old Stone Age) people, who lived nomadic lives as hunters and gatherers. By roughly 5000 B.C., they had developed settled communities, living in mud houses and practicing crude agriculture. These Neolithic (New Stone Age) people were probably the precursors of many of the modern inhabitants. "It is probable," writes British scholar James Parkes, "that remnants of the Neolithic population form part of the ancestry of the present Arab-speaking population, as well as the Jewish people of today."

The recorded history of the region, as pieced together from ancient Egyptian and Babylonian sources, began with migrations from the east that took place in the second millenium before the Christian era. Shortly before 2000 B.C., a nomadic people called the Amorites—a people skilled in making pottery and fashioning copper into tools and weapons—arrived in Palestine from the western edges of the great Arabian desert. They settled down, intermarried with the earlier people, and were regarded by the neighboring Egyptians as a troublesome, turbulent group. In other parts of Palestine lived the Canaanites, a pagan, idolatrous people who worshiped the cruel god Moloch and practiced human sacrifice. Such was the state of affairs in the region when the Hebrews arrived from the northeast around 1800 B.C.

THE COVENANT

Who were these Hebrews? Here we must backtrack a little and look at the monumental figure of Abraham, whose name in Hebrew means "Father of the People." The story of Abraham, his descendants, and their stead-fast belief in one supreme God is told in the Old Testament of the Bible. Originally, the story was handed down orally from generation to generation. The first five Books of the Old Testament—Genesis, Exodus, Leviticus, Numbers, and Deuteronomy—were not actually written down until the period between the ninth and fifth centuries B.C., many hundreds of years after the events they narrate.

According to Genesis, the first Book in the Bible, Abraham lived in the cosmopolitan Babylonian city of Ur, on the banks of the Euphrates. Around the year 2000 B.C., for reasons that are unclear, Abraham and his family decided to leave the city. They crossed the river and headed northwest, thus becoming the first people in the Bible identified as *Ivriim*—or in English, "Hebrews"— the people "who crossed over" or the people "from the other side of the river."

According to the Bible, Abraham and his people wandered some 600 miles (1,000 km) to the town of Haran, in what is now Turkey. There Abraham, now a seventy-five-year-old patriarch, had an experience that has reverberated down through the centuries and, incredibly enough, affects the Palestine question in our time. In Haran, says the Book of Genesis, Abraham encountered God (Jehovah) for the first time. The two entered into a Covenant, or pact. If Abraham would fol-

[5]

low God's commandments, then He, in His turn, would make the descendants of Abraham his "Chosen People." The God of Abraham made a single demand. All males among his Chosen People must be circumcised on the eighth day after birth, or, if converted into the faith, circumcised on conversion. In return, God promised that the land of Canaan would belong to the descendants of Abraham.

Accordingly, Abraham and his followers moved southward, into and around the territory of the Canaanites. On two further occasions, Abraham was again assured by God that his people—who would become "as numerous as the dust of the earth"—would inherit the land. But for quite some time, Abraham and then his successors wandered around in the vicinity of Canaan; they were nomads without a territory of their own. Then, around the sixteenth century B.C., a great famine afflicted the land, and so the hunger-stricken Hebrews migrated southward into Egypt. There, as Genesis tells it, Joseph, a great-grandson of Abraham who had been sold into slavery in Egypt by his jealous brothers, had risen to high rank in the pharaoh's court. Joseph interceded in behalf of his people. As a result, the peculiar newcomers with their odd belief in only one God were allowed to remain, multiply, and prosper.

KINGDOM AND CAPTIVITY
Some time later, perhaps after a century or two, new rulers took a different view of the alien Hebrews and made them slaves. It is quite likely that they formed part of the slave brigades that worked on the construction of some of the pyramids. No one knows how long the Hebrews were slaves in Egypt. But the biblical story of Exodus tells how God commanded Moses to lead His Chosen People out of Egyptian bondage and back into Canaan. Moses, though brought up in the Egyptian court (some scholars believe he may have been an Egyptian), assumed the role of leader of

[6]

the Hebrews and led them out of Egypt and into the Sinai Desert. In that arid land, they wandered for forty years, during which time Moses received divine law in the form of the Ten Commandments.

These Commandments have become part of the world's religious heritage. The Bible relates that Moses climbed cloud-wreathed Mount Sinai and had a personal encounter with God. There God gave Moses two stone tablets with the Commandments carved on them. Moses then presented his people with the God-given message— a message considered by people of differing religious faiths as one of the most lofty guides to how man should conduct himself on earth.

Moses died before he could lead his followers back to the Promised Land. It was left to his successor, Joshua, to take the Israelites, as they now called themselves, back into Canaan, where around the twelfth century B.C. they conquered the idolotrous inhabitants, abandoned their nomadic ways, and settled down. The term "Israelite" derives from a biblical story about Jacob, one of Abraham's grandsons. According to the Old Testament, God changed Jacob's name to Israel, from the Hebrew *Yisro-El*, meaning "Man who fought God," because Jacob engaged in a mysterious nighttime struggle with an unearthly being. To honor Jacob, his followers proudly called themselves Israelites.

For a time, the Israelites were weak and divided, but around 1000 B.C. they were forged into a kingdom by a strong leader, King Saul. His successor, King David, extended the frontiers by conquest and made Jerusalem the political capital. It was David's son and successor, King Solomon, who built the First Temple in Jerusalem in the tenth century B.C. On Solomon's death, however, the kingdom collapsed. After less than two hundred years, it dissolved into the feuding Hebrew kingdoms of Judah and Israel. To avoid confusion, it should be explained that the word "Jew" is a modification of *Yehu-*

[7]

di, a Hebrew term meaning "a citizen of Judah." The word "Jew" will be used here as a synonym for "Hebrew" or "Israelite."

In 721 B.C., the Assyrians, a warlike people from what is now Turkey, invaded the northern Jewish kingdom of Israel and destroyed part of it. The southern kingdom of Judah continued to exist, but the handwriting was on the wall. The Babylonians, who succeeded the Assyrians as the major power in southwest Asia, attacked Judah and in 586 B.C. they took Jerusalem after a six-month siege. Solomon's Temple was destroyed and the city reduced to rubble. Every Jew, with the exception of the poor, sick and crippled, was deported to Babylon, beginning what is known as the "Babylonian captivity" of the Children of Abraham. But the Jews did not forget Jerusalem—or "Zion," as they also called it. In the eloquent words of Psalm 137:

> By the waters of Babylon, we sat down,
> Yes, we wept when we remembered Zion.
>
> ....
>
> If I forget thee, O Jerusalem,
> Let my right hand forget its cunning. . . .
> Let my tongue cleave to the roof of my mouth.
>
> ....

EXILE AND RETURN

The exile in Babylon was the first major scattering of the Jews. It lasted only about fifty years, and during that time the exiles did not undergo great hardship. Babylon was ruled by a succession of enlightened kings who treated their captives with great tolerance. They respected the Jews as a special people because of their belief in one invisible God—a highly sophisticated concept at that time—and because of their strict moral code. By some accounts, those who lamented by the waters of Babylon were the minority; most of the Jews liked the

[8]

country, prospered in it, and were influenced by Babylonian, and later by Persian, culture.

Mighty Babylon fell to Cyrus the Great of Persia at the end of the sixth century B.C. Cyrus, too, respected the Jews, and he decreed that all who wished to return to Palestine would be permitted to do so. Some, but by no means all, of the exiles from Judah accepted the offer and returned to the Promised Land. There, after joining with the small number of Jews who had remained behind after the Babylonian conquest, they built a Second Temple in Jerusalem and lived as subjects of the Persian empire.

In the fourth century B.C., the Persians were defeated by Alexander the Great, giving the Greeks control of large parts of western Asia, including Palestine. Alexander, who had great esteem for the Jews, permitted them complete religious freedom and granted them a considerable amount of self-government. On his death, the vast empire he created by his military conquests was dismembered by his quarrelsome generals, and Palestine was ruled for almost two hundred years by a succession of kings with ties to Greece. Eventually, however, the Greek rule became oppressive, and in 165 B.C. the Jews rose in revolt. The leaders of this revolt, known as the Maccabees (from the Hebrew word for "hammer"), fought with incredible determination, for it was a religious war. As they saw it, they were fighting for their belief in God. The Jews took Jerusalem and purged the Temple of Greek idols. The Chosen People were once again dominant in Palestine—but not for long.

MASADA

In 63 B.C., the Roman General Pompey marched his powerful legions into the Maccabeean kingdom of Judah, subdued it, and renamed the country Judea. For more than a century, the Jews lived under Roman rule, bitterly resentful of the authorities' attempts to paganize

[9]

them. Finally, in A.D. 66, the angry Jews stormed a Roman garrison outside Jerusalem and routed the soldiers stationed there. Soon, the whole country was in open rebellion against the huge and powerful Roman empire. For three years, the Romans were kept at bay, but powerful new legions were rushed in from Europe. In A.D. 70, Jerusalem fell to the Roman armies. Amid tremendous fires and streets literally drenched with blood, the Romans plundered and slaughtered.

In the midst of this defeat, however, a Jewish force held out at the stronghold of Masada, a towering plateau overlooking the western bank of the Dead Sea. The Jewish defenders numbered about a thousand, but the tiny force stubbornly held off a large Roman army throughout the winter of A.D. 72–73. When it became clear that the Romans were about to break into the fortress, the defenders made a pact with one another: not one man, woman, or child would be taken alive. They burned their possessions and then systematically committed suicide. When the Romans finally burst into the Masada fortress, only two women and five children remained alive. According to the historian Josephus, the leader of the Jews on Masada, Eleazar ben Yair, told his followers before their suicide: "I cannot but esteem it as a favor that God hath granted us, that it is still in our power to die bravely and in a state of freedom."

Many thousands of Jews perished in this first Jewish-Roman war, but a good number of Jewish settlements managed to survive. The Romans used the Jews to work the land or fill minor administrative posts. But the Jews remained rebellious and in A.D. 132 another revolt erupted. Under the daring leadership of Simon ben Cozeba, better known as Bar Cochba ("Son of the Star"), the Jews retook Jerusalem and inflicted other humiliating defeats on the Romans. This time, the Emperor Hadrian resolved to punish the Jews severely.

He recalled his best general, Severus, from Britain and put him at the head of 100,000 elite troops. Bar Cochba's men could not resist this juggernaut, and in the year 135 the Romans overwhelmed the rebels, almost totally destroying Jerusalem. Among other things, they forbade Jews ever again to set foot in the city.

In the wake of Bar Cochba's defeat, many Jews fled to Asia and Africa. Captive Jews were taken back to Europe and sold as slaves; many thousands were slain in gladiatorial games in Rome. Judea became a province of Rome and was renamed Palestina, part of a larger province, "Syria Palestina." The Jewish population of the region was decimated, and the vast majority of Jews was scattered to the far corners of a Roman empire that stretched from Britain to India. The great Jewish Diaspora—or "scattering"—was to last for many centuries, indeed up until our own times. But down through those long centuries, Palestine remained the emotional home-land—the Promised Land—of the Jews.

For the time being, however, the Roman legions ruled in Palestine. Jupiter and his fellow pagan gods had temporarily supplanted Jehovah. But matters were to grow even more complicated. The religion of Jesus of Nazareth, who was born a Jew and considered by his followers to be the long-awaited Hebrew Messiah, gained huge numbers of adherents throughout the Roman empire in the third and fourth centuries. So great was the appeal of the creed of Jesus that the Emperor Constantine made Christianity the official religion of the empire in the early fourth century. As a result, Christianity became the dominant religious faith in Roman-governed Palestine and continued to dominate the region until well into the seventh century. By then, a new era was about to dawn in Palestine—an era that would be dominated by people emerging from the silent reaches of the Arabian desert.

3

The Rise of Islam

For countless centuries, the sun-drenched expanse of the Arabian Desert, the world's largest peninsula, was the homeland of Bedouin and Quraish Arabs. The Bedouins were desert dwellers; the Quraish congregated on the coast, where they established small trading villages. Neither group made much of a mark on history until well into the Christian era. Like many primitive people, the Arabs were nature worshipers. Stars, trees, stones, inanimate objects of all kinds, were held in extreme reverence. Chief among the objects of veneration was a black meteorite, the Black Stone, enshrined in the Kaaba ("cube") in Mecca.

In the early centuries of the Christian era, however, new ideas began to infiltrate Arabia. Travelers along the coast spread word of the mighty empires and great prophets of the world. Jews fleeing Palestine after the Roman victory in A.D. 135 settled in coastal Arabia, gradually spreading some knowledge of the Old Testament and the concept of monotheism. Under the influence of these sophisticated ideas, the Arabs were soon to explode as a political and cultural force.

[12]

THE MESSENGER OF GOD

Around the year 570, a child who was to become one of the most remarkable men in history was born in Mecca. This was Mohammed, a name which means "highly praised," and he and his followers would radically change and religious and political landscape of the Middle East, Africa, and parts of Europe and Asia. The influence of Mohammed remains pervasive into the twentieth century. After fourteen centuries, he continues to dominate the thinking of the many millions in the Muslim world, including the Arab population under Israeli rule and the Palestinian Arabs who live in exile, as the Jews did long before them.

Mohammed was born into the prominent Quraish clan, but both of his parents died before he was six, and he was brought up in poverty by his grandfather and later by a Bedouin nurse. He was never taught to read or write. Little is known of his youth, except that at the age of twelve or thirteen he traveled to Syria as a camel driver in a caravan. In Syria, he was exposed to the Jewish and Christian religions for the first time—and the young man was deeply impressed. He developed deep respect for Jews, whom he called "the people of the book," and for Christians as well. The Hebrew patriarchs and Jesus became his religious mentors; his contempt grew for the primitive religious practices of his fellow Arabs.

At the age of twenty-four, Mohammed married an older woman, a rich widow named Khadija, and became a successful merchant. But material success was not enough for him. Mohammed was distressed by the paganism he saw around him—and also by the lack of any sense of Arab nationhood. He dreamed of uniting the many tribes of Arabia into an Arab nation and of having a monotheistic religion on a level with Judaism or Christianity. Often he would retreat into the mountains near Mecca to mediate and pray.

[13]

One night in a cave on Mt. Hira, God manifested Himself to Mohammed in the form of the Archangel Gabriel. In a scene reminiscent of Moses on Mount Sinai, Mohammed said that Gabriel showed him a tablet. Although Mohammed was illiterate, he read the tablet at the angel's command. The message was that Allah was the one true God and that Mohammed was designated as His messenger on earth. Shaken by the experience, Mohammed questioned his own mental stability. But after a period of hesitation, he began to preach the religion of Allah.

Studded with references to Jewish and Christian doctrine, Mohammed's message was a fervent proclamation of the unlimited power of the one God, the Creator of the universe, who would summon all creatures into His presence for judgment on the day of resurrection. All living beings were responsible to Allah, a God of mercy as well as justice, for their own actions. Everyone must show a love for Allah through faith, prayer, and charity. In his preaching, Mohammed freely acknowledged his debt to the prophetic tradition of the Jews and Christians; he gave special praise to earlier apostles of monotheism—particularly Abraham, Moses, and Jesus.

At first, Mohammed preached only to his family and friends but then a widening circle of Meccans began to listen to Allah's self-proclaimed prophet. Slowly at first, then with astonishing speed, more and more accepted the new faith. A convert became known as a Muslim, "one who surrenders" to the will of Allah. The name of the religion, Islam, means "submission to the will of God." Like the Christians before him, Mohammed made many of his early converts among the lower classes and slaves, the underprivileged of the Arab world.

FLIGHT TO MEDINA
Mohammed dictated his messages and prophecies to scribes, or secretaries, who put them down in the holy

[14]

book, the Koran, which literally means "Recitation." Shortly after his death, devout followers added to the body of Muslim doctrine with the *sira*, a biography of their leader. They recorded Mohammed's pronouncements, other than those in the Koran, in a work called the *hadith*.

Mohammed's growing popularity among the poor of Mecca aroused suspicions among the prosperous, who saw him as a dangerous radical. And so, in A.D. 622, fearful of being harmed by his opponents, he fled to Medina, 200 miles (320 km) to the north. There was a Jewish community in Medina, and there Mohammed hoped to win Jewish converts to his own monotheistic doctrines. To his distress, the Jews rejected his claim to be a successor of Moses; in retaliation, Mohammed and his followers seized the money and goods of the Jews. Then, the Prophet used the wealth to raise an army of 10,000 and march on his enemies in Mecca. They capitulated quickly and Mohammed entered the city, where he ordered all pagan idols to be smashed. Mohammed not only had an appealing message, he had a winning army. Within a few years, all of Arabia came under the sway of the new religion, Islam.

Mohammed considered Jews and Christians infidels, or nonbelievers, but he allowed them to practice their religions openly, in return for a payment of tax. Muslims were instructed to say to Jews and Christians: "We have faith in that which has been revealed to us and in that which has been revealed to you. Our God and your God are one, and unto Him we are resigned."

THE CONQUERING SWORD
Before Mohammed died in 632, Muslim rule had spread with remarkable swiftness to parts of North Africa and western Asia. His influence spread even more rapidly after his death. Just as he was the "Conquering Word of Allah," his friend and successor as Muslim leader, Abu

[15]

Bakr, was the "Conquering Sword." Islam was on the march. In the years that followed, the troops of Abu Bakr—who was called the Caliph, or "successor"—raided Iraq and Syria and defeated Byzantine troops in southern Palestine. The chaotic, warring tribes of Mohammed's youth had become an invincible army. On their lips was the cry: "No God but Allah; Mohammed is the Messenger of Allah."

Within a century, the scimitar spread Islam and Arab culture to half the known world, including large parts of Asia and North Africa. By 711, the Muslims were established as far west as Spain and as far east as Indonesia. In the west they were checked only by the Pyrenees Mountains and by the Frankish king Charles Martel, who defeated them at Tours in 732. In the eastern part of Europe, they were blocked for a time by the Byzantine empire, ruled from Constantinople. But for centuries, Arab power and culture were to reign supreme in a vast part of the known world, while Europe endured the miseries of the Dark Ages.

ARAB PALESTINE

Palestine also came under Arab sway. By 638, the Muslims had overrun the entire country. Many of the inhabitants there were unhappy with the rule of the Byzantine empire and welcomed the Arab invaders. After a long siege, Jerusalem fell to the Arabs; its surrender was received by the Caliph Omar—Abu Bakr's successor and an early convert of Mohammed. Omar was a devout follower of the faith and regarded Jerusalem as a particularly holy place because years before Mohammed himself had proclaimed the city to be holy ground. The Koran tells how Mohammed, astride a miraculous winged steed with the face of a woman and the tail of a peacock, was taken one night during his sleep in his home in Mecca to the site of the former Jewish Temple in Jerusalem and thence to heaven for a meeting with Allah.

When Caliph Omar entered Jerusalem, he asked the

Byzantine authorities to be shown the place from which Mohammed made his ascent to heaven. Omar was shocked to find it in a filthy state, a place for dumping garbage. He ordered the place cleaned, and at the end of the Old Temple platform he built a simple structure for Muslim worship. Years later, in 691, the Muslim rulers built the beautifully graceful Dome of the Rock, or the Mosque of Omar, near the same spot. For that reason, the Muslims hold Jerusalem as the third most sacred city, behind Mecca and Medina.

Under Omar and his successors, Christians were allowed to retain their places of worship and Jews were allowed to return to the city of Jerusalem. At the time, a majority of the population was Christian; a small minority was Jewish. The Muslim rulers regarded both groups as entitled to protection under the law but not to full equality. The Jewish and Christian infidels were allowed to retain their property and their religious practices. But they were not allowed to build new religious buildings, dress like Muslims, or appear to be on an equal footing with Muslims. They were excluded from service in the armed forces.

Over the years, many of the Christians in Palestine converted to Islam and became Arabized. Christians, however, remained a majority in the country until around the beginning of the ninth century; after that date the majority of the inhabitants of Palestine were Arab and Muslim. Many Bedouin Arabs from the desert had moved in and settled down in the friendly climate of a country dominated by their ethnic brethren.

The Jews in Muslim-ruled Palestine, as in other parts of the Arab empire, fared better than they had under the Byzantine Christians. The Arabs regarded the Jews, along with the Greeks and Persians, as elite people worthy of respect. The Jews were literate, the Jews respected learning, the Jews kept their strict moral code. From about A.D. 700 to roughly A.D. 1000, a Jewish "Golden Age" flourished in the Muslim world. Learned
[17]

Jews made important contributions in almost every field of study. Jerusalem, Tiberias, Haifa, and Gaza became centers of sacred Jewish studies that often existed on money sent by fellow Jews living thousands of miles away.

By the eleventh century, however, the Muslim empire had begun to disintegrate. Arab rule in the Palestine area ended in 1071, and with it ended an era of relative tolerance and enlightenment toward the Jews. From that date, the country fell under the control of erratic and sometimes brutal rulers—the Seljuk Turks, the Christian Crusaders, the Mongols from Asia, and the Mamelukes from Egypt who ruled Palestine from 1260 until 1517. The Ottoman Turks (from Othman, a warrior who founded a new Turkish empire in the fourteenth century) entered this rich historical pageant when they drove the Mamelukes out of Palestine in 1517. The Ottoman Turks were to remain in control of the Holy Land until the end of World War I. Interestingly enough, all of these conquerors, with the exception of the Mongols and Crusaders, were non-Arab peoples who had adopted the religion of Islam, but the population of Palestine remained heavily Muslim—and Arab.

The era of the Crusades was a particularly terrible one for both the Jews and the Muslims of Palestine. In Palestine ostensibly to free the Holy Land from the infidel Turks, the Crusaders left a trail of plunder, rape, torture, and murder across the land. They slaughtered both Muslims and Jews, and their barbaric actions nearly led to the total extinction of the Jews in Palestine.

Once the Crusaders had gone back to Europe, the Jews were permitted by later rulers of Palestine to cluster in small communities in the cities, particularly in Jerusalem, where they often lived in squalid conditions, but they—and their fellow Jews in the Diaspora—continued to dream of the day when Jerusalem once again would be the center of a proud Jewish state.

4

Diaspora in Europe

With their defeats at the hands of the Romans in the first century B.C. and the first century A.D., the Jews found themselves scattered throughout Europe—some as involuntary exiles, some as slaves, some as people seeking greener pastures. But they were always aliens, sometimes persecuted, sometimes welcomed. Indeed, their survival in Europe is one of the most gripping stories in history.

Despite the two Jewish-Roman wars, in A.D. 212 the Emperor Caracalla granted the Jews who now flooded his realm extraordinary rights. He assured them of full equality under the law and even granted them Roman citizenship. This policy changed when the Emperor Constantine recognized the Christian Church as the only legal church in 324, but even then the rights of Jews were only limited, not entirely revoked. Jewish men were later forbidden to marry gentile women, a prohibition that did not perturb them, or to hold public office, a prohibition that was a minor annoyance. By and large, the early centuries of the Christian era in Europe were not a period of great hardship or suffering for most Jews.

The fifth century brought havoc to Europe. Wave after wave of barbarians from Asia—Goths and Vandals, Franks and Huns—swept down on the decaying Roman Empire and brought terror and destruction to Christian and Jew alike. In time, the once-mighty empire, rotting in its political and social decadence, totally collapsed. But the barbarians certainly did not, in any historic terms, emerge as the masters of Europe. Exhausted and finally defeated, they were absorbed into the older European populations. Most became Christians and pillars of the church.

FEUDALISM AND THE JEWS

With the end of the Roman Empire, the feudal age took root in Europe; new nations—now known as Italy, France, Spain, and Germany—were evolving; the Christian Church was the dominant institution. In this Christian world, the Jews—literate and sophisticated—often provided the scholars and merchants, the judges and magistrates.

A chief reason for the general hospitality shown the Jews was the feudal system itself. Feudalism provided for only three classes—the nobles, who fought and governed; the priests, who tended to religious life; and the serfs, who did the manual work. Someone had to become the merchants, artisans, and moneylenders, and so this was left to the Jews, who existed largely outside the feudal system. The Jews thus became the forerunners of the later "middle class."

Known for their learning and business acumen, Jews were invited by local authorities to settle in Italian cities. In the ninth century, Charlemagne invited them into France and Germany in order to build commerce and minor industry. The emperor gave the Jews a liberal charter of self-government and awarded them high posts in his court. Except in Spain, where they were forced to convert to Christianity or die, Jews lived tranquil, prosperous lives in the early Middle Ages. And even Spain adopted a more lenient attitude after the Muslim conquest of the eighth century. Until the eleventh century, the Church itself was tolerant of the Jews, hoping that time would cure what it considered their obstinate refusal to accept Jesus, one of their own, as the Messiah. But far more difficult times lay ahead for the Jews of the European Diaspora.

ANTI-JEWISH FEELING

In the twelfth and thirteenth centuries, the Crusades— originally launched to take the Holy Land from the Turks—became a nightmare for the Jews. In order to gain soldiers for the eight Crusades, most of which were disastrous failures, freedom was offered to serfs, pardons were given to criminals, and absolution was granted to sinners. Thus, in addition to some dedicated Christians, the ranks of the Crusaders included large numbers of riffraff who were far more interested in pillage than in piety. On their road of march, they foreshadowed their barbaric conduct in the Holy Land by sacking thousands of Jewish settlements, looting, raping, and killing with total impunity. Estimates are that the Crusaders, fired with hostility toward all non-Christians, paused to kill about 100,000 Jews on their way to Palestine.

A factor in this anti-Jewish climate was a change in the attitude of the Church. Once reasonably tolerant, Church officials in Rome lost patience with the people who, by refusing to convert, presented people with alternative beliefs. This, the Church fathers feared, could encourage dissent against official doctrine among Christians. At the Fourth Lateran Council, called by Pope Innocent III in 1215, laws designed to isolate the Jews from the general community were enacted. Among other things, Jews were required to wear badges on their clothing to identify them as Jews. Popular feeling against the Jews began to rise dangerously, sparking attacks on Jews and their homes. Accusing Jews of the ritual murder of Christian children, hysterical mobs destroyed syna-

[21]

gogues and burned copies of the Talmud, the holy book codifying Jewish law.

In addition to the ignorant mobs, a growing Christian middle class began to criticize the large number of Jews in trade and moneylending. It was precisely these areas of business that the rising Christian middle class wanted to take over for itself. And so the anti-Jewish pressures mounted. In 1290, England—where Jews had lived since 1066, when William the Conqueror invited them to settle—became the first western country to expel the Jews. By the fourteenth century they were banished from France; in the fifteenth century, some of the German states forced the Jews to leave.

RENAISSANCE, INQUISITION, AND REFORMATION

The years of the Renaissance (roughly 1320–1520) brought a glorious flowering of the arts and sciences in western Europe. But the Church's response to the outpouring of imagination and inquiry was to severely chastise those suspected of heretical thought. The Inquisition, an office of the Catholic Church dedicated to the special task of finding and punishing heresy among Christians, did not apply to the Jews, since they never professed the Christian faith. As a result, the Jews by and large escaped the inquisitorial flames that claimed so many Christian lives in Europe. In Spain, however, those Jews who had converted to Christianity in earlier centuries, the so-called Marranos, were fair game for the heresy-hunters. Many Marranos were tortured and led to the fiery stake.

Tomás de Torquemada, leader of the Inquisition in Spain, was not able to harm Jews who never professed Christianity, but he hated Jews so much that he bullied Queen Isabella and King Ferdinand into ordering the expulsion of all Jews in 1492. At the time, the 1500-year-old Jewish community in Spain was 150,000 strong; of these, around 50,000 chose conversion instead of

[22]

expulsion. The others left their homes and sought havens in more tolerant lands. On the very day that Columbus set sail for the New World, his ships passed vessels in the harbor of Palos loaded with unhappy Jewish refugees headed for unknown new homes. In 1496, Portugal threatened to enact anti-Jewish laws, creating an atmosphere that sent many more Jews fleeing to the corners of the earth.

By the early years of the sixteenth century, the Jews had all but disappeared from western Europe, once the center of their life. Most Spanish and Portuguese Jews chose to settle in North Africa or the Middle East, Muslim lands where they enjoyed a great measure of religious and economic freedom. The exiles from England, France, and parts of Germany moved farther east, to eastern Germany, Austria, Poland, and Lithuania, where they were welcomed at first for their skills and learning. Eastern Europe became the center of Jewish life.

During the sixteenth century, the armies of the Reformation (Protestants) and the Counter Reformation (Catholics) engaged in bloody warfare in the name of religion. Both sides strove for the support of the Jews, who wisely kept their heads down and waited for the fighting to end. When it did end, after the Thirty Years War (1618–1648), western Europe was divided into Protestant and Catholic states. The Protestant states, such as England, were mercantile states; they invited the Jews back to join in the task of building capitalism. The Catholic states, largely agricultural and more conservative, did not extend the invitation. In any event, most of the Jews chose to remain in the *shtetls* ("villages") and *ghettos* ("walled city neighborhoods") of eastern Europe—not always under the best of circumstances.

POGROMS, PEASANTS, AND COSSACKS

Jewish life in eastern Europe was uncertain at best, dangerous at worst. At first the rulers of Poland, Prussia,

[23]

and Russia had welcomed the newcomers in hopes that they would introduce advanced trade, commercial, and banking practices to their backward lands. But by the fifteenth century, the ill fortune that befell the Jews in the west began to pursue them eastward. The old ritual-murder charges were raised once again. The first *pogroms*, or organized mob attacks on Jews, broke out around 1500 in Poland and continued sporadically during the sixteenth century.

For a time, it seemed that the efforts by some princes and some churchmen to save the Jews from violence had defused the explosive situation. But the oppressed peasants of eastern Europe hated the nobles, hated Jews who worked for the nobles, and hated many of the well-to-do clergy. They were waiting for the moment to exact the greatest revenge.

That moment came in 1648, when a band of Greek Orthodox Cossacks, living in border areas between Turkey and Poland, rebelled against the nobles and Roman Catholic Church of Poland. These Cossacks, led by a merciless chieftain named Bogdan Chmielnicki, were soon joined by Polish peasants eager for vengeance. For ten years, Cossacks and peasants terrorized the countryside, carrying out acts of unprecedented brutality. Nobles, priests, and Jews were tortured, mutilated, and murdered. No one knows for certain how many people died, but seven hundred Jewish communities in Poland were totally wiped out. Estimates are that as many as 100,000 Jews died in this savage uprising.

PROGRESS IN THE WEST, PERSECUTION IN THE EAST

In the eighteenth century, Poland was invaded by Russia and partitioned by Russia, Prussia, and Austria. The Jews of Poland were now the subjects of new rulers. The Russians did not want them but did not know what to do with them, so Jewish settlement was limited to a strip of territory along the western border called the "Pale of

[24]

Settlement." Despite this policy, some Jews drifted out of the Pale and into some of the larger cities.

In Prussia and Austria, anti-Jewish discrimination was sporadic. In those countries, as in Italy and France, many Jews prospered greatly; some, who were occasionally derided as "Court Jews," rose to become influential advisers to powerful political figures.

The more excessive stages of the French Revolution created panic among some wealthy Jews, but many others applauded the revolution's call for *liberté, egalité, fraternité*. The rise of Napoleon Bonaparte was also welcomed by most Jews. To Jews and Christians alike, the French military genius was a liberator whose armies smashed oppressive old regimes in Europe. Jews took note that, wherever his armies moved, the ghetto walls came tumbling down.

In western Europe, as the nineteenth century progressed, Jews enjoyed the same rights and privileges as their gentile fellow-citizens. By and large, the Jewish communities enjoyed a high standard of living and many Jews rose to high positions in business, banking, and government. The brilliant Benjamin Disraeli, a Jew, became prime minister of England and one of the most powerful men in Europe.

But if the Jews of western Europe flourished, those in central and eastern Europe underwent difficult times. In Russia, under a series of repressive or erratic tsars, most Jews sank into profound poverty and despair. In the last decade of the nineteenth century, tens of thousands of Jews were massacred by peasants who themselves were living in squalor and desperation. The peasants murdered the Jews; the tsarist government, anxious to see a decline in the Jewish population, did little to prevent the violence. These Russian governments also looked on complacently as Jews were robbed or driven from their homes.

Faced with such persecution, Jews fled Russia in record numbers—perhaps as many as three million—for lands where anti-Semitism was less ugly and brutal. Many found new homes in western Europe, but most of them packed up their pitiful possessions and shipped out in steerage for the New World. During the fifty years from 1870 to 1920, the Jewish population of the United States exploded from 250,000 to four and a half million. An exodus to Palestine, the biblical homeland, also took place, although on a smaller scale. Before 1880, only about 12,000 Jews—chiefly religious people, students, and small businessmen—lived in Palestine. By 1914, the Jewish population of Palestine had climbed to 80,000, and many of these newcomers were an entirely different breed. The new immigrants hoped to work on the land, make a living as farmers, and perhaps help one day to create a Jewish homeland.

A NEW KIND OF ZIONISM
This longing to return to Palestine had been kept alive in the hearts of European Jews down through the centuries. For most of that time, however, the concept of a "return to Zion" was primarily a religious impulse. Religious Zionism was named for King David's "Hill of Zion," a symbol for Jerusalem and all Palestine. But these religious Zionists believed that a return could come about only when a "Messiah" appeared to lead the way.

Because of the persecution of Jews in eastern Europe in the late nineteenth century, Jewish political thinkers came to revise this concept of Zionism. "Why wait for a Messiah, when suffering Jews needed immediate help?" they asked. Jewish intellectuals like Leo Pinsker and Theodore Herzl began to think that it was impossible for Jews to assimilate in European society. Moreover, they argued that it was not even desirable to assimilate, since their unique Jewishness inevitably would be lost. The Jews, these political Zionists reasoned, needed their own homeland, where they could rebuild Jewish religious and cultural values, revive the

[26]

Hebrew language and provide a safe refuge for Jews from every part of the world.

Herzl, in particular, rallied world Jewry behind the banner of political Zionism. A brilliant Viennese journalist and playwright, Herzl became increasingly disgusted with the anti-Semitism he saw around him in Europe. In 1896, he published his historic book *Der Judenstaat* ("The Jewish State"), and in it he argued the case for a mass return of Jews to the ancient homeland of Palestine. The book generated great excitement in Jewish communities in Europe and America. Many Jewish assimilationists, those who wished to blend into the societies in which they lived, regarded Herzl as a troublemaker; but many, particularly in the poorer Jewish communities of eastern Europe, were stirred by his vision of a Jewish revival in Palestine. They called Herzl *Herzl ha-Melech*—"Herzl the King" of the future Jewish state.

In 1897, Herzl organized the first World Zionist Congress in Basle, Switzerland. Few non-Jews took note of this event, but it was the beginning of an organized drive by world Jewry to carry out Herzl's ideas. In 1901, the Jewish National Fund was established to purchase land for Jewish settlers in Palestine, and Zionists of every nationality donated money, even hard-earned pennies. Gradually, in the early years of the twentieth century, the Fund began to acquire land, sometimes at exorbitant prices, from Arab or Turkish owners. Jewish communities began to grow; parts of the country that had not been cultivated for centuries suddenly became green with fields and orchards.

Before 1880, there had been only 12,000 Jews in Palestine. By the outbreak of World War I in 1914, the Jews in the country numbered 80,000 as against 700,000 Arabs. The Jewish communities were mere drops in the Arab ocean. Neither the Turkish rulers, nor the Arab majority, could have dreamed what the future held in store for Palestine.

5

The Mandate Years

The last decades of the nineteenth century and the early years of this century witnessed a strong revival of nationalism in many parts of the Arab world. After centuries of quiet subjection to the Turks, intellectual ferment and political dissent appeared on all sides. Young Arabs, many of them influenced by American, British, and French educators and missionaries, discovered the glories of the Arab past. Many dreamed of—and planned for—emancipation from the Turks. The Arabs of Palestine were no different. They wanted their own independent state, and with the decline in Turkish power they could see the feasibility of attaining that goal. But at the same time, they also began to perceive a potential threat to that dream of nationhood: the Zionist movement and the growth of the Jewish population in their midst.

World War I proved to be crucially important to the future of the Middle East—and to Palestine in particular. The Sultan of Turkey threw in his lot with the Central Powers (Germany and the Austro-Hungarian empire) against the Allied Powers (Britain, France, Belgium, Russia, and Serbia, later joined by Italy and the United States). It proved to be a monumental blunder by the Sultan.

[28]

BRITISH PROMISES

When the fighting began in 1914, Arab nationalists were uncertain where their interests lay. Some favored supporting Turkey in the hope of winning a degree of Arab autonomy after the war. Others wished to side with the Allies, gambling that victory for them could lead to the creation of a series of independent Arab states. Reports of Turkish atrocities against Arabs under their rule drove many Arabs into the Allied camp. British promises of postwar independence for the Arabs did the rest.

In an exchange of letters in October 1915 between Sir Henry McMahon, the British high commissioner in Cairo, and Sherif Hussein, a spokesman designated by the Arabs, the British held out promise of Arab independence after the war. McMahon had been given the authority to speak for the British government, which wanted to gain the Arabs' support and also spark an Arab uprising against Turkey. But the imprecision in the letters left the ultimate disposition of Palestine in a state of uncertainty. To this day, however, the Arabs contend that the McMahon-Hussein letters amounted to a direct British promise to create independent Arab states in the Turkish empire, including one in Palestine.

There can be no doubt that at the time the Arabs were satisfied with McMahon's assurances. Living up to their part of the bargain, they revolted against Turkey in June 1916. Sherif Hussein troops seized a number of Turkish outposts in the Arabian Peninsula, while his camel-back troops harassed Turkish lines of communication and transportation. While not large in numbers, the Arab troops were strategically important, since they diverted Turkish troops and supplies and stirred anti-Turkish feeling among Arabs throughout the Middle East. In 1917, the Arab forces fought with British General Edmund Allenby when he invaded Palestine, defeated a Turkish army, and seized Jerusalem.

But if the British were eager to win Arab support during World War I, they were just as eager to win favor

[29]

with Jewish public opinion in Europe and the United States. The Jewish community in the United States was of particular importance, since Britain wanted the United States to enter the war and wanted every bit of support it could get in American public opinion. The Germans were bidding for support among international Jewry; the British had to counter the German effort. Zionists in London, confident of an Allied victory, were all too willing to respond to Britain's friendly overtures.

THE BALFOUR DECLARATION

A key role in Zionist dealings with the British was played by Chaim Weizmann, a distinguished British chemist and an ardent Zionist with close ties to important figures in the government of David Lloyd George. Soon after the outbreak of war in 1914, the British government called in Weizmann for secret talks and asked him to take on a critically important task: the development of synthetic cordite, an explosive vital to the country's war effort. Prior to the war, Britain made the explosive from acetone, a substance it had imported from Germany. With Germany now on the other side of the battlefield, Britain had to produce a substitute. Weizmann set to work, successfully discovered a method of producing synthetic cordite, and turned it over to the British government.

As a result, the British government could hardly turn down Weizmann when he asked it for some expression of support for the establishment of a Jewish national home in Palestine. Such a concept appealed on religious grounds to many highly placed Britons, schooled as they were in the Bible. Other important people in London, including top military strategists, believed that a substantial future Jewish population in Palestine with strong ties to Britain would add to the security of the crucial Suez Canal area.

Against this background, on November 2, 1917,

Foreign Secretary Arthur Balfour, a strong pro-Zionist though not a Jew, wrote a letter to Lord Lionel Walter Rothschild, a wealthy and influential Zionist. In it, Balfour made what was later termed the Balfour Declaration. It stated that "His Majesty's Government views with favor the establishment in Palestine of a national home for the Jewish people." This was qualified by the statement that "nothing shall be done which may prejudice the civil and religious rights of existing non-Jewish communities." The declaration was approved in advance, but not without doubts, by the U.S. president, Woodrow Wilson. After all, the Arabs were the vast majority of the population of Palestine, and Wilson above all stood for the principles of independence, self-determination, and democracy based on the will of the people. But the American president became convinced by the British government that the Balfour Declaration did not threaten the rights of the majority. In 1918, the declaration was also approved by France and Italy, two other leading members of the wartime alliance.

The Balfour Declaration was less than a total triumph for the Zionists, since it did not endorse the view that all of Palestine should be considered a Jewish homeland. It made no mention of a Jewish state. The declaration's support for *a* national home *in* Palestine, when looked at carefully, actually promised very little. But it went far enough to create jubilation in the camp of the Zionists, who saw it as an important step toward the establishment someday of a Jewish state.

The Arabs were stunned. Their leadership had not been consulted about the Balfour Declaration. Then came another heavy blow when reports surfaced that the British and the French had signed a secret wartime agreement that totally conflicted with the promise of Arab independence made by McMahon. The Sykes-Picot Agreement, named after the chief British and French negotiators, carved up Arab-inhabited lands in the soon-to-be-defeated Turkish empire into British and French spheres of influence. A sense of total betrayal gripped the Arabs.

POSTWAR ARRANGEMENTS

Britain tried to mollify Arab leaders, including Sherif Hussein, assuring them that the Sykes-Picot Agreement was not a formal treaty and that the settlement envisaged in the Balfour Declaration would be limited and would not lead to the creation of a Jewish state. London left the Arabs with the impression, as a later Royal Commission put it, "that the British were going to set up an independent Arab state which would include Palestine." Weizmann also soothed the Arabs by assuring them that the Zionists did not seek political power in Palestine. For a time, the Arabs swallowed their suspicions.

After the war, the Allies thoroughly dismembered the Ottoman empire, leaving Turkey a much-reduced and weakened republic. Independent kingdoms were created in the Arabian Peninsula. For certain Arab-populated areas, which theoretically were not ready for self-government, the Allies imposed what they called a "mandate system." Under this arrangement, each newly established political entity was to be put under the control of one of the Allies, which was to govern it for a stated time under the overall supervision of the newly formed League of Nations. France, for example, was given the mandate for Syria and Lebanon; Britain, the mandate for Iraq and Palestine. (See map, p. 50.)

Britain assumed the Palestine mandate in 1920 and under an agreement with the League of Nations the Balfour Declaration was made part of Britain's mandate. The strongly pro-Zionist agreement between Britain and the League recognized the "historical connection of the Jewish people with Palestine." It called for the easing of restrictions on Jewish immigration and the "close settlement by Jews on the land," provided that the rights of "other sections of the population are not prejudiced." At
[32]

the time, the "other sections of the population" of Palestine—the Arabs—made up nearly 90 percent of the inhabitants.

The London government named Sir Herbert Samuel as first high commissioner for Palestine. Samuel was a highly esteemed British Jew with powerful political connections, and his appointment was seen by Zionists as a sign that the British mandatory power would give Jews preferred treatment in Palestine. In Zionist quarters in parts of eastern Europe, the Balfour Declaration by now had become a near-sacred document; Sir Herbert's picture was hung reverently in shop windows from Danzig to Sverdlovsk. Encouraged by what they heard about Britain's attitude, Jews by the thousands—mostly from eastern Europe—packed up and left for Palestine.

ARAB RESENTMENT

As Jewish immigration quickened and the number of Jewish settlements and institutions multiplied, resentment against Zionism, the British, and the Jews flared among the Arabs of Palestine. "Whose land is it?" asked the Arabs. After all, Arabs formed the vast majority of the population, and Arabs had been the dominant population group in Palestine from the seventh to the twentieth century. Was this not a stronger historical claim than that of the Jews, which was based on a much shorter occupation that ended almost 2,000 years ago?

The Jews, of course, saw things in an entirely different light. They believed they had a historic, biblical claim to the land promised to them by God. Zionists also argued that Jews had suffered much in the Diaspora and that only a homeland would provide a haven against persecution. What about the rights of the Arabs? Zionists maintained, possibly with some merit, that a large influx of Jews into Palestine would benefit the population by introducing higher levels of skill and education.

It was hard to dispute the fact that the Zionist settlers were beginning to transform Palestine. The Jews rebuilt old cities and constructed new ones; they established rural settlements, irrigated the desert land and made it bloom with citrus groves; they brought science and modern methods to agriculture, medicine, and sanitation. They also introduced the essentially alien concept of the kibbutz, an agricultural collective in which people shared the fruits of their labor; some of the collectives tried, not always successfully, to apply pure communal principles and discard the habit of private property.

The achievements of the Jews, however, served only to anger many Arabs. After all, their ancestors had lived for centuries under Turkish rule, kept in ignorance, unused to self-rule, and now incapable of defending their own land against these interlopers. Moreover, the Arabs argued, the advanced Jewish techniques did not benefit them. Most Jewish-owned industries at that time excluded Arab workers; land sold by an Arab (usually at an inflated price) to a Jew, according to Zionist practice, could never revert to Arab ownership. In addition, the Arabs believed that the Jews were insensitive and arrogant. These were some of the arguments against Jewish immigration. Meanwhile, the reality was that Jewish settlers continued to arrive and Arab hostility continued to mount.

In April 1920, in the first outbreak of violence, five Jews were killed and two hundred eleven wounded during a three-day riot in Jerusalem. In May 1921, more violence erupted, resulting in the death of forty-seven Jews and forty-eight Arabs, the latter killed by British police trying to protect the Jews. To pacify the Arabs, Sir Herbert Samuel temporarily suspended Jewish immigration, but it was soon resumed and Jewish newcomers continued to pour in and settle on land purchased for them with funds from Zionist organizations in Europe and America. During the years from 1922 to 1926, 75,000 more Jews arrived in Palestine, nearly doubling the Jewish population and greatly increasing the number of Jewish settlements.

As more boatloads of Jewish settlers arrived and more Jewish settlements sprouted, frustrated Arabs saw their hopes for an independent Arab state in Palestine slipping through their fingers. The British rulers used every kind of tactic to calm Arab nerves. In July 1922, Britain issued a statement of policy known as the Churchill Memorandum, after the then colonial secretary, Winston Churchill. It assured the Arabs that "the disappearance or the subordination of the Arabic population, language or culture" was not contemplated by Britain. It said that the Jewish national home promised in the Balfour Declaration would not mean "the imposition of a Jewish nationality upon the inhabitants of Palestine as a whole, but rather the further development of the existing Jewish community." To further appease the Arabs, the Churchill Memorandum also quoted a statement by Zionist leaders to the effect that they wanted nothing more than for the "Jewish people to live with the Arab people on terms of unity and mutual respect."

Despite these British assurances to the Arabs, more and more boatloads of Jewish immigrants continued to arrive in Palestine, and Arab anger rose at the thought of eventually becoming a minority in their own country. In 1929, this Arab frustration led to the most serious anti-Jewish rioting yet seen under the British Mandate. It began with a simple incident, the blowing by Jews of the *shofar*, the ceremonial ram's horn at the Western ("Wailing") Wall in Jerusalem on Yom Kippur, the Jewish Day of Atonement. This was contrary to custom and British law, since the wall—the sole surviving part of the Second Temple, destroyed by the Romans—was adjacent to the revered Muslim holy place, the Dome of the Rock. Arab religious zealots quickly accused the Jews of encroaching on this holy site, with the aim of destroying the Mosque and rebuilding the Temple.

The violence that began in Jerusalem soon spread throughout the country as howling Arab mobs invaded Jewish communities, burning, looting, and killing. By the time the British authorities brought the disturbances under control, 133 Jews lay dead and a great amount of Jewish property was destroyed.

The British, who had tried to please both sides, first soothing the Arabs, then the Jews, were caught in an impossible situation. Both sides accused the mandatory power of duplicity. The Arabs believed that the British supported the Zionist cause and that they were using the Zionists as an entering wedge in a complicated plan to absorb Palestine into the British empire. Among the Jews, the belief grew that Britain was reneging on a commitment to the goals of Zionism. Moreover, the Jews suspected that some members of the British administration in Palestine, particularly among the police, harbored anti-Jewish sentiments and sympathized with the Arabs.

The 1929 rioting altered Jewish attitudes toward self-defense. From that point on, the Jews were convinced that they would have to defend themselves instead of relying on the British authorities. Early in the 1920s, the British had armed and trained a special Jewish police group to help them protect Jewish agricultural settlements against Arab raiders. As the Arab-Israeli troubles became more serious, this legal group was slowly transformed into an illegal, secret Jewish underground army called the Haganah. It took its orders from the Jewish leadership, not from the British. In the early 1930s, it greatly strengthened its manpower, weaponry, and training, all with funds from the Jewish communities of Europe and America. The lines were being sharply drawn between Jew and Arab; and the Jews clearly were preparing for what seemed to be an inevitable major confrontation.

THE NAZI IMPACT
Still, the situation in Palestine might have been stabilized, except for an event that was to have a major impact on the whole world: the coming to power of Adolf

[36]

Hitler and the Nazis in Germany in 1933. The anti-Semitic laws enacted by the Nazis and the menacing growth of anti-Semitism in central Europe gave new impetus to the Zionist movement and caused many European Jews to seek sanctuary in Palestine. Immigration by Jews reached new peaks, increasing the total Jewish population in the Holy Land to 400,000. These new migrants were not land-tillers, merchants, or holy men. Many were sophisticated German Jews who had escaped Hitler's horror with skills, knowledge, and money. Many were highly educated scientists, artists, professionals, and businessmen—people who brought added substance to the growing Jewish community.

In reaction to the swift growth of the Jewish community, the embittered Arabs again took to the streets to demonstrate their unhappiness. Between 1936 and 1939, the Arabs staged a series of bloody anti-Jewish, anti-British riots. These soon began to look like a full-scale Arab revolt. Terrorists operating under the leadership of Haj Amin al-Husseini, holder of the religious title of grand mufti of Jerusalem, assassinated British officials and police officers, derailed trains, set oil pipelines afire, and attacked Jewish settlements. Arabs who cooperated with the British authorities were kidnaped, tried by kangaroo courts, and killed.

The British were unable to control the increasingly chaotic situation. Hoping to mollify the Arabs, in 1939 the British government of Prime Minister Neville Chamberlain issued a White Paper which placed strict limitations on Jewish immigration to Palestine. At the time, the Jewish population had climbed to half a million—against roughly twice as many Arabs. Under the White Paper, Jewish immigration would be restricted to 75,000 over the following five years; thereafter, quotas for Jewish immigration would be dependent on the consent of the Arabs. Stringent restrictions would be placed on land sales to Jews in certain areas and complete prohibition in others.

[37]

ZIONIST OUTRAGE

Not surprisingly, this policy provoked bitter protests in the Zionist ranks. Many feared it would close the door to many Jews in Nazi Germany who hoped to find refuge in the Holy Land. At this point, some irate Jews directed their guns at the British. The extremist Irgun Zvai Leumi ("National Military Group"), formed a few years earlier by a former Russian-Jewish journalist named Vladimir Jabotinsky, now began to play a key role. The Irgun, a secret paramilitary group that believed in direct, violent action, blew up the Palestine broadcasting station at the very moment the announcement of the White Paper was scheduled to be made. During the days that followed, Irgun terrorists killed a policeman, fired shots in Arab neighborhoods, and exploded bombs in telephone booths, Arab houses, and the Department of Migration. The world at large had heard of the Irgun for the first time; it would not be the last.

More moderate Jews in Palestine were also angry at the British. The chief rabbi of the country tore up a copy of the White Paper in the main synagogue in Jerusalem. Jews throughout the country took an oath not to tolerate the new British policy, while Zionist organizations made plans for a massive illegal immigration.

With the outbreak of war against Nazi Germany in 1939, however, Jews of all political views closed ranks behind Britain and its allies. The first objective was the defeat of Nazi Germany, and during the war the Zionist organizations helped recruit 43,000 Palestinian Jews for military service with the British. These Jews wanted to help defeat Hitler, but they also wanted to gain the military experience they would need for the inevitable postwar confrontation with the Arabs. The Zionists knew that a clash was inevitable because they were prepared to exert every pressure on the British and on world opinion for the establishment of a Jewish state once the war was over. And, quite correctly, they anticipated that the Arabs would resist such a development.

[38]

There can be little doubt that Jews benefited greatly from the military training they received from the British in World War II. And, strangely enough, not only those Jews who served in regular British units were the beneficiaries. Although the Haganah was still regarded by the British authorities in Palestine as an illegal army, Prime Minister Winston Churchill actually had British intelligence operatives—members of the Special Operations Executive (SOE)—work behind the scenes to train Haganah members in the use of such modern weapons as plastic explosives. These British undercover agents actually helped to form the Palmach, the elite commando force of the Haganah, and supplied it with money and arms. In return, the Haganah carried out secret attacks into Lebanon and Syria, then under the control of the Nazi-controlled government of occupied France; they also interrogated Jews who escaped Nazi-occupied Europe and passed along intelligence to British agents.

All this went on behind the back of the nominal British authorities in Jerusalem. Says Israeli statesman Abba Eban, who then served as the link man between Haganah and SOE: "It was strange, because the basic policy was to disarm Jews, whereas here was a British organization trying to make them as armed and tough as possible. . . . Jews would be picked up by the police for carrying arms and it would be my job to sort the imbroglio out. I would appear with my SOE identity card and explain that these were people allowed by SOE to carry arms. My SOE card could get them released."

The Palestinian Arabs, like Arabs everywhere, played little role in World War II. Many were sympathetic to the Allied war effort. But some of them, like the grand mufti of Jerusalem and his followers, helped the Germans with intelligence about British operations in the Middle East. These Arabs hoped that a British defeat would somehow lead to an independent Arab Palestine, but the effect of their pro-German actions was to tarnish the Palestinian cause in the eyes of the world.

[39]

6

Birth
of a Nation

Only after the total collapse of Germany in 1945 did the
world learn the full extent of the atrocities performed by
the Nazis. American, British, and Soviet troops liberated
death camps at Dachau, Buchenwald, and Belsen that
were piled high with corpses. The smell of burning flesh
still lingered around the ominous smokestacks as survivors, many barely alive themselves, told shocked battle
veterans what had happened. The Nazis had systematically rounded up political opponents and people of "inferior stock," and murdered men, women, and children
by gassing, shooting or any means available. Among the
more than 12 million victims were between 5 and 6 million Jews. Quite rightly, Jews around the world called
it—and still call it—the Holocaust.

BRITISH IMMIGRATION POLICY
Huge numbers of Jewish survivors needed new places to
live in safety, but many Western countries imposed tight
legal restrictions on immigration of any kind. As a result,
Zionists mounted a worldwide publicity campaign,
aimed particularly at public opinion in the United States
and Britain, to get the London government to repudiate
the White Paper of 1939. Jewish organizations spared no

[40]

effort in lobbying for their point of view. They wanted unlimited emigration rights to Palestine for survivors of the Nazi regime and support for the establishment of a Jewish state in Palestine.

Jews hoped that the victory of the British Labor party in the elections of July 1945 would open the doors of Palestine to Jewish immigration. Labor had, in the past, consistently supported the Zionist cause. Once in power, however, the leaders of the Labor party had to take a hard look at world realities. First, the British economy, after years of war, was in tatters; Britain was in debt to the Arab states and was heavily dependent on them for oil. Second, many Labor party leaders feared the expansion of Soviet influence in the Middle East. To protect Britain's vital interests in the region, the new government reasoned, it would have to keep on the good side of the Arabs. For these reasons, Clement Attlee's Labor government stunned the Zionists by retaining the 1939 White Paper as policy, thereby severely restricting Jewish settlement and land purchase in Palestine.

Under strong pressure from American Zionists, and also because he was genuinely moved by the plight of the survivors of the Holocaust, U.S. President Harry Truman pleaded with the British to admit 100,000 Jews into Palestine immediately. When Britain refused for fear of offending the Arabs, Zionist organizations bought ships and transported Jews from Europe to Palestine, where tens of thousands of illegal immigrants made their way into the country despite British coastal patrols. Some of the ships were intercepted by the British and taken to Cyprus, where their passengers were placed in detention camps. In a show of exasperation, the British sent one ship, the *Exodus*, back to Europe with its 4,500 desperate passengers.

The story of the *Exodus*, which occurred in July 1947, commanded worldwide attention at the time. When the ship reached the waters of Palestine after a journey from Genoa, it was intercepted by British patrol

[41]

boats. When the British tried to board the *Exodus*, the angry passengers—chiefly refugees from Germany and Poland—attacked them with buckets, bottles, crowbars, and even cans of food. In the ensuing melee, three of the refugees were killed before the British gained control of the ship. They brought the badly battered *Exodus* into Haifa harbor and had to drag the still-resisting refugees off the ship for transfer to another vessel, the *Empire Rival*. As Abba Eban, the Israeli statesman, later wrote: "The Jewish refugees had decided not to accept banishment with docility. If anyone had wanted to know what Churchill meant by a 'squalid war,' he would have found out by watching British soldiers using rifle butts, hose pipes and tear gas against the survivors of the death camps."

On orders from London, the *Empire Rival* first sailed to Port du Bouc in southern France, where the refugees refused to leave the ship. It then sailed to Hamburg, where they cursed and spat upon the British troops who forced them to disembark on the hated German soil from which most of them had fled. From Hamburg, the refugees were taken to a Displaced Persons Camp at Poppendorf, where they remained until they could migrate "legally" to Palestine or elsewhere. The *Exodus* affair caused an international uproar and made British immigration policy seem heartless. It also generated considerable sympathy for the Zionist cause.

Enraged by British policy, the Jews of Palestine turned increasingly militant. The Irgun had maintained a truce with Britain since the start of the war against Germany, but in 1945—under a new commander, a recent arrival from Poland named Menachem Begin—the terrorist band was eager for action. Beginning with mortar attacks on police stations and raids on arms depots, the Irgun stepped up its campaign of violence as the year progressed. Its raiders attacked railway yards and Royal Air Force installations. They gunned down British soldiers in the streets.

[42]

The most spectacular act of Irgun terrorism came in July 1946 when three men dressed in Arab clothing arrived at the King David Hotel in Jerusalem. The King David was headquarters for the British army, but—since it was the main hotel in Jerusalem and open to the public—there was little military security. The three intruders carried three milk churns loaded with explosives. These they placed in the cellar and hooked up with detonators and timing devices. Then they fled. A short time later, a huge explosion rocked the King David.

When the smoke cleared and the rubble was removed, ninety-one British officers and men lay dead; another forty-five were wounded.

The King David affair infuriated British public opinion and the British authorities in Palestine. A crackdown against the Jewish underground was mounted; many arrests were made and terrorist arms caches unearthed. But new guns always appeared, and the shooting went on. When the British hanged a number of convicted Irgun terrorists, the Irgun shocked the world by hanging two captured British soldiers.

The Irgun was not the only Jewish illegal military force striking at the British. The Haganah, which formerly disdained such attacks and concentrated on building its regular units, now launched some raids of its own. Haganah men raided the camp for illegal immigrants at Athlit, cut through the wire and released the inmates. In another exploit, the Haganah exploded several hundred devices all over Palestine, causing 242 breaks in the railway network. The Palmach, the underground army's crack commando units, blew up two police launches in Haifa harbor and one in Jaffa.

THE UN PARTITION

By 1947, the British had had enough. Harassed by the Jewish underground, pressured by the Zionists, criticized by an increasingly pro-Zionist President Truman, and reviled by the Arabs, the London government was ready

[43]

to wash its hands of Palestine forever. The United Nations had succeeded the defunct League of Nations as overseer of the mandatory powers, and so the British referred the seemingly insoluble question to the United Nations and hoped for the best. The United Nations quickly established a Special Committee on Palestine, usually known by its initials as UNSCOP.

In months of hearings in Jerusalem, Beirut, New York, and Geneva, the eleven-nation committee studied hundreds of reports and documents; it held hearings with many Arab and Jewish leaders. In the end, it proposed the creation of two separate, independent states, one Arab and one Jewish, with the city of Jerusalem and its environs to be placed under an international authority operated by the United Nations (see map, p. 50). The UN plan also envisaged an economic union—an arrangement which would encourage trade and commercial relations—between the two countries. On November 29, 1947, the UN General Assembly accepted the proposal of UNSCOP and voted, by thirty-three to thirteen, with ten abstentions, for the partition plan.

The Arabs hotly opposed the Assembly's action on the grounds that it would divide the country, against the wishes of a majority of its population—the Palestinian Arabs. The Palestinian Arabs themselves vowed never to accept a partitioned Palestine. On the other hand, the Zionists strongly welcomed the partition scheme; so did the United States, most Western countries, and the Soviet Union. The Zionists, in particular, had reason to celebrate. After decades of activity that sometimes must have seemed futile, the world body had recognized their right to a state in Palestine for the Jews. In addition, the Jews were to receive fifty-five percent of the country's territory, although they remained a distinct minority of the population.

One Jew who rejoiced at the UN vote was a young Haganah officer named Moshe Dayan, later to become a general, defense minister, and political leader in Israel. Dayan wrote in his memoirs: "I felt in my bones the victory of Judaism, which for two thousand years of exile from the Land of Israel had withstood persecutions, the Spanish Inquisition, pogroms, anti-Jewish decrees, restrictions, and the mass slaughter by the Nazis in our own generation, and had reached the fulfillment of its age-old yearning—the return to a free and independent Zion." Dayan went on: "We were happy that night, and we danced, and our hearts went out to every nation whose UN representative had voted in favor of the resolution. . . . We danced—but we knew that ahead of us lay the battlefield."

Dayan's superiors agreed with his assessment. In the months after the passage of the UN resolution, the Haganah swiftly prepared itself for the conventional war it knew was coming, building its arms supplies and recruiting Jews with military experience from every part of the world—including the United States and Europe. Most of the Haganah's troops were deployed along the Syrian border, where the Arab military threat seemed to be greatest. Technically, the Haganah was still an illegal army, but it gradually began to operate openly and the British by now had little interest in suppressing it.

Meanwhile, Palestine was in complete chaos. The happy British prepared to leave, the eager Jews prepared for statehood, and the angry Arabs were bent on disruption. Relations between Arab and Jew had become almost unbearably tense. In areas where ordinary Jews and Arabs lived elbow to elbow, shoving matches, rock-throwing duels, and gun battles became common occurrences. Arab terrorists, inflamed by antipartition agitators, attacked Jewish men, women, and children all over the country. In the twelve days following the UN vote, they burned Jewish buses on the highways, looted Jewish shops, and killed eighty Jews.

The Jewish underground was also active, with the

Irgun, as usual, carrying out the most shocking acts. In a calculated attempt to frighten Arabs into flight, Irgun terrorists entered the Arab village of Deir Yasin on April 9, 1948, and proceeded to massacre its inhabitants. Irgunists riddled the village with bullets and threw grenades into the stone houses, where civilians huddled in terror. There was no Arab military presence in the village. When the Irgun raiders left Deir Yasin, they left behind 250 dead men, women, and children.

It was a deed remembered with the greatest bitterness by Arab Palestinians to this day. Menachem Begin, who ordered the Irgun raid on Deir Yasin, became Israel's prime minister in 1977; Begin has refused to admit that his men acted unjustly or cruelly. Other accounts, dating back to 1948, including those of the International Red Cross and the Jewish leadership at the time, confirm that the Irgun had committed a repugnant atrocity. The events at Deir Yasin and attacks on other Arab villages sent some 300,000 Arabs into headlong flight across the borders into neighboring Jordan, Syria, and Lebanon.

THE BRITISH DEPART

On May 14, 1948, in accord with the UN resolution, the British—to their great relief—hauled down the Union Jack and departed from Palestine. Exhausted by the war against Germany, hated by Jews and Arabs alike, the British had simply proved unable to solve the conflict in Palestine. To be sure, the British were far from blameless. They had promised the Jews a national homeland and seemed to have promised the Arabs an independent Palestinian state in the same territory. First they encouraged Jewish immigration, then they discouraged it. One day they placated the Jews, the next day they placated the Arabs. It was, all told, a disaster for British policy.

Their final moments in Palestine were humiliating

for the British. When General Sir Alan Cunningham, Britain's top official in the final period, left Government House for an aircraft that would carry him back to Britain, he had to ride in a specially built bulletproof Daimler with windows an inch (2.54 cm) thick. Cunningham later recalled: "We drove through Jerusalem with Jews on one side and Arabs on the other, all pointing guns, but they let me through."

That afternoon, the state of Israel was born as Zionist leaders proclaimed the creation of a Jewish state— eighteen hundred years after the defeat of Bar Cochba by the Romans had scattered the Jews to all parts of the world. "My eyes filled with tears and my hands shook," recalled Golda Meir, later to become prime minister of Israel. "We had done it. We had brought the Jewish state into existence."

The Jews did not have much time to celebrate. Next day, on May 15, the armies of Egypt, Jordan, Iraq, Syria, and Lebanon, who had pledged to fight for an Arab Palestine, launched an invasion, touching off the first Arab-Israeli war. In the first weeks of the fighting the Arab armies performed quite well, taking the offensive and occupying areas which, for the most part, had been allotted to the Palestinian Arabs in the UN partition plan. The Arabs of Palestine, who were badly organized, poorly armed and totally ready to let the armed forces of the neighboring Arab states do the fighting, contributed little to the actual battle. They did, however, supply intelligence about Israeli movements to the Arab armies and commit random acts of sabotage against the Israelis, such as cutting telephone lines and blowing up bridges.

The Israelis, who initially suffered from a shortage of arms, were on the defensive, fighting desperately while they attempted to strengthen and equip their forces. The Arab armies drove west of Jerusalem to within 10 miles (16 km) of the Mediterranean, threatening to cut Israel in half. The situation, Israeli spokesmen admitted, sometimes verged on the catastrophic. It was, indeed, a critical moment for the Israelis. To gain time, they turned to the United Nations and asked it to arrange for a cease-fire. After the United Nations threatened to impose economic sanctions on them if they did not accept a cease-fire, the Arabs—against their better judgment—agreed to a four-week truce.

The truce resolution banned the introduction of new manpower or weaponry into the area; but both sides ignored the UN restrictions. During the four-week interval, however, the Israelis were more successful than the Arabs in building their military strength. The United States and western Europe had placed an embargo on the sale of all arms to either party, but Israel—with considerable foresight—had made an arms deal with Czechoslovakia. During the truce period, an airlift from Czechoslovakia delivered to the Israelis an enormous supply of rifles, machine guns, artillery, and tanks. When the truce was over, the Israelis were ready.

CHANGING TIDE

In the opening days of the second round, the Arabs—confident of their strength—moved forward on most fronts. Then they suddenly ran into Israeli troops who had the arms and equipment they lacked at first. The Israelis not only repulsed the Arabs but, to the world's surprise, began to advance. This time it was the Arabs who called for a truce, which was negotiated by UN mediator Count Folke Bernadotte of Sweden. But peace definitely was not in the cards. Both sides violated the cease-fire shamelessly, building their military power as best they could. In the fall of 1948, fighting flared sporadically as Bernadotte tried to find a solution. Some Jews considered the UN diplomat to be pro-Arab, apparently because he suggested that the Palestinian refugees who fled to other countries during the fighting be allowed to return to their homes. On September 17, Jewish extremists—probably members of a notorious terrorist group called the Stern Gang—shot and killed Bernadotte in Jerusalem.

The Israelis, well armed and more confident now, bolstered by volunteers who had served in the armed forces of the Allies during World War II, started their own offensive. The Arab armies, hampered by long supply lines and the lack of a unified command, began to crumble. The Israelis advanced on almost all fronts and even pushed a short distance into Egyptian territory in the Sinai. Calls for an armistice came from the United Nations, the United States, and western Europe; Israel—though it had the military advantage now—agreed. An armistice was signed on July 30, 1949. Under its terms, Israel significantly expanded the territory it had originally been awarded under the United Nations partition plan of 1947.

As the result of the fighting, Israel gained the following territories (see map, p. 50) that were to have been part of the Palestinian Arab state envisaged by the United Nations: sizable areas in the southern Negev Desert; parts of the Gaza Strip—the sliver of land along the Mediterranean coast that contains the Arab city of Gaza; and a large chunk of the northern region of Galilee. The Israelis also won the newer quarters of Jerusalem; under the UN partition plan, the entire city of Jerusalem would have been under international jurisdiction.

On the Arab side, only King Hussein's Jordanian army had acquitted itself at all well in the end. During the war, the Jordanians had crossed the Jordan River and occupied the West Bank area. This region also was to have been part of the Palestinian Arab state. In addition, after fierce fighting with the Israelis, the Jordanians seized control of the largely Arab-inhabited part of Jerusalem known as the Old City. That sector of the city contains such important religious sites as the Jewish

[49]

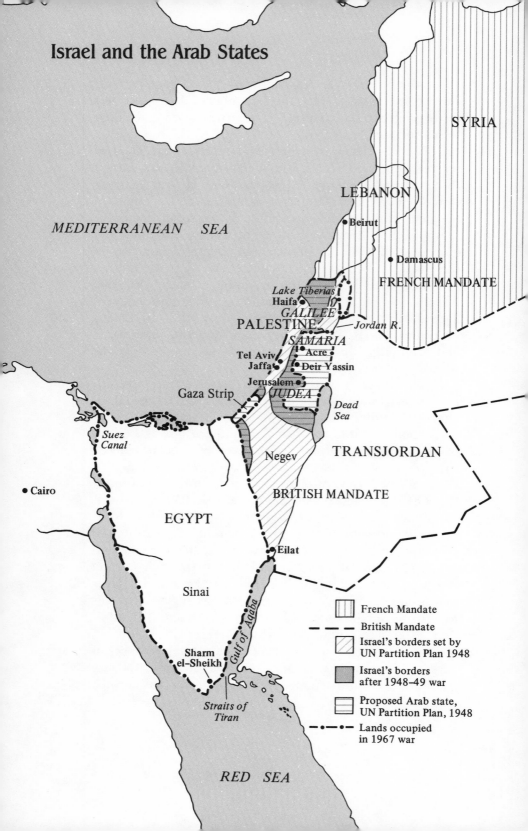

Israel and the Arab States

SYRIA

LEBANON

• Beirut

MEDITERRANEAN   SEA

• Damascus

FRENCH MANDATE

Lake Tiberias
Haifa•
GALILEE

PALESTINE

Jordan R.

SAMARIA

Tel Aviv•   •Acre
Jaffa•   •Deir Yassin

Jerusalem•
Gaza Strip   *JUDEA*

*Dead
Sea*

Suez
Canal

Negev   TRANSJORDAN

• Cairo

BRITISH MANDATE

EGYPT

•Eilat

Sinai

Gulf of Aqaba

Sharm
el-Sheikh

*Straits of
Tiran*

RED   SEA

	French Mandate
	British Mandate
	Israel's borders set by UN Partition Plan 1948
	Israel's borders after 1948–49 war
	Proposed Arab state, UN Partition Plan, 1948
	Lands occupied in 1967 war

Western ("Wailing") Wall, the only existing remnant of the Second Temple, destroyed by the Romans in the first century A.D.; the Christian Church of the Holy Sepulchre; and the Muslim Dome of the Rock Mosque. As a result of the fighting, the city of Jerusalem was divided, and it was to remain divided by barbed wire and armed Israeli and Jordanian patrols for the next eighteen years.

In its first military encounter with the Arabs, Israel had won an impressive victory. It gained more territory and now had room for more immigrants. But the victory was not just a matter of territory. The war showed the Israelis that they could fight and win against what was originally perceived to be enormous odds. The war did nothing less than assure the continued existence of the Jewish state.

The Arabs had taken a bad beating. The Arab states, which had confidently expected to oust the new Israeli state from the land of Palestine, failed dismally. For the Palestinian Arabs, particularly, the loss to the Israelis signaled the beginning of a long nightmare. Many of them had been forced to leave their ancestral homes and olive groves and flee the country. They not only did not see Israel driven into the sea, as they had expected, they witnessed an expansion of Israeli territory. At the end of the 1948 war, Palestine was partitioned all right, but between the Israelis and Jordanians. The hapless Palestinian Arabs had nothing.

7

Israelis and Palestinians

Israel had survived its first major challenge—but not its last. In the next quarter of a century, the Jewish state became the most powerful military force in the Middle East. But most Arabs, and particularly the Palestinians, were far from resigned to Israel's existence.

THE INGATHERING

On independence day, the Jews of Palestine—now the Israelis—installed a preplanned temporary government, which lasted eight months. Bullets were still flying in the War of Independence when the first national elections were held on January 25, 1949. A profusion of parties, from religious groups to communists, contested the election. In the voting, a democratic socialist, pro-western party named MAPAI (the Workers Party of Israel) emerged as the dominant political force. With its allies, MAPAI controlled the Knesset (parliament); its leader, David Ben-Gurion, a Zionist who had fought for decades for the establishment of a Jewish state, was chosen as the first prime minister. In one of his first official utterances, Ben-Gurion declared that Zionism was dead, having "committed suicide" by its success in gaining the independent state of Israel.

[52]

The new state faced tremendous problems, and high on the list was the "Ingathering of the Exiles"—the vast number of Jews from around the world who wished to come to Israel. The essence of the Zionist movement, after all, was the creation of a state whose doors would be open to every Jew. Now, the uprooted Jews of Europe and Jews from Muslim lands were quick to take advantage of the opportunity. They came by land and sea; those who could do neither were airlifted to Israel in what was called "Operation Magic Carpet."

As a result of this new wave of immigration, the population of the tiny new country almost trebled in the first four years following independence: from 665,000 in May 1948, to over 1,600,000 by May 1952. Almost all these newcomers were poor and unskilled; they had to be given housing and work; and they had to adapt to life in a totally different land. But to most of them, it was a dream come true.

THE JEWISH STATE

The state established in 1948 is structurally a democracy. All Israelis, whether Jew, Arab, or Christian, have the right to vote. In fact, there usually are a few Palestinian Arab members of parliament.

Yet, Israel is, by its own definition, a "Jewish state." In a cogent commentary Terence Smith, former *New York Times* bureau chief in Jerusalem, wrote in 1975:

"Legally, the Arabs are full-fledged Israeli citizens with the same rights and duties as the 2.6 million Jewish residents of the state. They vote, they sit in parliament, they own land, run businesses, go to their own public schools, hold union cards, participate in the national health scheme, carry Israeli passports and, occasionally, even die in the same indiscriminate terrorist attacks in the streets of Jerusalem.

"There are two exceptions to this legal equality: Israeli Arabs are not called to serve in the armed forces on the ground that it is unreasonable to expect them to

[53]

take up arms against their fellow Arabs, and their kin are not entitled to automatic Israeli citizenship, as [the relatives of] Jews are, under the Law of Return. This automatically confers citizenship upon Jews who migrate to Israel but does not apply to non-Jews."

But the legal status of the Palestinian Arabs in Israel is only part of the story. In many other ways, they have been treated as second-class citizens—in part perhaps because of their own shortcomings, in part because of Israeli attitudes.

After the 1948 war, the new state of Israel did not have much trouble with the Palestinians who chose not to flee. Only a few hundred thousand remained, and they were rural peasants concentrated in the western and central portions of Galilee, where there were few Jews. As a result, there was little contact between the Israeli Arabs (Palestinians) and the Israeli Jews. Little attempt was made to absorb the Israeli Arabs into the Israeli mainstream; the Arabs had their own schools, they spoke their own language, and they maintained their own culture. A separate Arab society developed within Israel, and it had little contact with the Jewish society.

It was an arrangement that successive Israeli governments found comfortable, even though it flew in the face of the old Zionist argument that a Jewish state would benefit the Arabs by their contact with more advanced western ways. As the years went by, the per capita income of the Palestinian Arabs in Israel remained markedly lower than that of even lower-income Jews. Few Arabs went to Israeli universities. Few, if any, Arabs became leading business, financial, or educational figures. Not one, not even a token Arab, was included in the higher echelons of the Israeli government.

One reason for all this, of course, is that the more educated, more affluent Palestinians had fled the country to pursue upward mobility elsewhere. But the Israeli establishment did not exactly hold out its hand to the Palestinian Arabs living in its midst. Arabic was an official language in Israel along with Hebrew, but few Israeli officials could speak it. There were no university courses in Arabic; if an Arab wanted to go to a university, he had to learn Hebrew.

The specifically Jewish nature of the Israeli state could also be seen in the powerful influence of the rabbinate—the body of leading Orthodox rabbis—and the bloc of religious parties in parliament. The religious establishment of Orthodox Judaism dictated what could and what could not be done on the Sabbath. It has dictated that Jews could not marry non-Jews in Israel, and it constantly tried to impose its views on such matters as education and the role of women in society. The religious establishment even put great pressure on the government to ground El Al, the country's airline, on the Sabbath, even though it would mean the loss of needed revenues.

The extent to which the government bowed to the Orthodox religious establishment was a constant irritant to secular-minded Israelis. So important was religion as an element in government that the state established a minister of religious affairs; the state also built synagogues and paid the salaries of rabbis, though Muslims and Christians were not given such favored treatment.

Under these circumstances, can Israel be called a democracy? The answer must be a qualified "Yes, but . . ." The fundamental basis of democracy is majority rule. Supposing the Palestinian Arabs living under Israeli rule one day outnumbered the Jews and were able to elect their own people to govern the land? This is not an outlandish concept given the high birthrate in the Arab community. Would this majority of Palestinian Arabs be permitted to govern? The answer is a short and simple "No." For Israel is, by definition, a Jewish state. Is such a concept compatible with democracy?

SHATTERED COMMUNITY
Smarting under their defeat in the 1948–49 war, the Arab states yearned for revenge. But they were not ready

[55]

to challenge Israel, with its growing arsenal of U.S.-supplied weaponry, on the battlefield. Instead, they chose economic measures to express support for the Palestinian Arabs. Even before Israeli independence, the Arab League—the loose umbrella organization of all the Arab states—had placed a boycott on goods produced by Jewish firms in Palestine. After the birth of Israel, the boycott was intensified; all types of economic, financial, and even personal contacts with Israel were prohibited. Foreign companies that did business in Israel were blacklisted in the Arab world. In 1951, the Arab League stepped up the pro-Palestinian boycott by trying—unsuccessfully, as it turned out—to cut off oil supplies to the Jewish state.

Thanks to massive economic and financial aid to Israel from Jews around the world, and thanks to substantial aid from the government of the United States, the boycott failed. The Israeli economy not only survived but made significant progress. Still, the Arab boycott, which cut off natural sources of raw materials and natural markets, posed a distinct hardship for a young nation trying to get its economy off the ground.

After 1948, the Palestinians, both those who had remained at home and the many more who had fled the country, were a shattered community. The defeat had come as a bitter shock, since they had been fully convinced that the intervening Arab armies would oust the Jews and set up an independent Arab state in all of Palestine. When this did not happen, the Palestinians heaped scorn on the Arab countries who had come to defeat the Israelis and failed. Still, the Palestinians were totally dependent on these Arab states, who were hopelessly at odds with each other and in no condition to venture another crusade in support of an Arab Palestine. At the same time, the Palestinians evinced little enthusiasm or any capacity for organizing themselves into a distinct movement.

In the early 1950s, Palestinian military action was

[56]

largely confined to small-scale incidents along the demarcation lines set by the armistice. Usually these were minor affairs, carried out by private individuals or groups, along the borders with Egypt, Jordan, and Syria. Over the years, however, the incidents grew in intensity and scope. In August 1955, after accusing the Egyptian army of helping terrorists slip across the border and bomb Israeli settlements, the Israelis launched short, punitive attacks against Egyptian outposts in the Gaza Strip. Israel also assaulted Syrian positions along the Sea of Galilee in December, drawing a rebuke from the UN Security Council for violating the armistice.

ISRAELI WARS,
PALESTINIAN PREPARATIONS

In the summer of 1956, the Israelis—eager to wipe out small Palestinian guerrilla nests and even more eager to show Egyptian strongman Gamal Abdel Nasser who was military boss of the region—rolled their tanks into the Sinai Desert and did not stop until they reached the Suez Canal. At the same time, Israel's co-conspirators in the venture, Britain and France, dropped airborne troops into key points in Egypt. The British and the French wanted to punish Nasser for nationalizing the Suez Canal, which had been owned by an Anglo-French consortium. The whole episode came to an ignominious end when U.S. President Dwight D. Eisenhower, irate at three American allies staging such an operation without consulting Washington, demanded that they withdraw their troops from Egyptian territory. They were in no position to argue with their all-powerful ally in Washington, and so, reluctantly, they withdrew.

During this period, the Palestinians seemed quiescent. But some Palestinian exiles, among them a pudgy young man named Yasir Arafat, were beginning to organize. In the oil sheikhdom of Kuwait, where he formed his own engineering firm, Arafat and his friends founded al-Fatah ("Victory") in 1959. He gained financial

[57]

backing from wealthy Palestinian exiles in Kuwait and arranged to have his followers trained in Algeria. By 1963, Arafat was ready for action; in that year he moved to Syria, which he used as a springboard for minor raids on Israel. He and his men, now numbering perhaps several hundred, also began to operate out of Jordan, and from there he launched a series of attention-getting raids in 1965. Actually, the al-Fatah raiders did little more than blow up some Israeli water installations, but they—and Yasir Arafat—had made the Israelis take notice.

Other developments affecting the Palestinians were afoot. In the late 1950s, high-level participants in Arab League meetings such as Egypt's President Nasser, constantly emphasized the need for the Palestinian Arabs to organize themselves in order to take the lead in the struggle against Israel and to form the political nucleus for a future Palestinian state. In an effort to help the Palestinians help themselves, the Arab League met in Cairo in 1964 and created the Palestine Liberation Organization; at its head the League placed the Palestinian Ahmed Shukairy.

But if Palestinians like Arafat and Shukairy finally were taking action in behalf of their own cause, many others still believed that only the Arab armies of Syria, Jordan, and Egypt had the capacity to defeat the Israelis and establish a Palestinian Arab state. Then came the Six-Day War in 1967 and further disillusionment for the Palestinians. In the fighting, the Israelis battered the Syrian, Jordanian, and Egyptian armies. In less than a week, they seized the Sinai peninsula, the Golan Heights of Syria, the West Bank of the Jordan, and the Old City of Jerusalem. (See map, p. 50.) Israel's crushing victory shook many Palestinians out of their earlier conviction that outside armies could present them with nationhood on a platter. Clearly, the time had come for Palestinians to take their fate into their own hands—or at least to make the attempt.

8

The Rise of the Palestine Liberation Organization

The years after the Six-Day War were to witness Yasir Arafat's assumption of PLO leadership and a significant growth in the guerrilla organization's operations and influence. Palestinians—whether living under Israeli control, in the refugee camps in Arab lands, or in countries scattered around the globe—came to accept the PLO as their legitimate representative. Many foreign governments accorded it diplomatic recognition; the United Nations granted it observer status.

THE DISPOSSESSED
A large part of the support for the anti-Israeli guerrillas came from the bitter inhabitants of the Palestinian refugee camps operated by the United Nations in Jordan, Lebanon, Syria, and Egypt. The violence before and during the 1948 war caused between half a million and 780,000 Palestinian Arabs to flee into the neighboring Arab states. The Six-Day War of 1967 added immensely to the problem, since more than 200,000 additional Palestinians flooded into the camps to join the earlier exiles.

When these camps were established by the UN Relief and Works Agency for Palestine Refugees in the

Near East (UNRWA) in December 1949, it was to have been a temporary measure. By May 1950, UNRWA had its program in operation, offering the refugees food, clothing and shelter, medical care, and education and vocational assistance. The expectation of UN officials at the time was that a combination of repatriation of the refugees to their old homes and resettlement in various Arab countries would solve the problem. That expectation proved to be totally unrealistic.

Over the years, Israel has steadfastly refused to accept any of the refugees back, on the grounds that it could not accommodate such a number of hostile people. Besides, Jewish immigrants occupied the lands once owned by the Palestinians. As far as resettlement was concerned, the Arab states had a mixed record. They were willing to absorb the small percentage of refugees who had skills or education. In fact, the skilled or educated quickly left the camps and found jobs in every part of the Arab world. At the same time, the Arab states were none too eager to take in the illiterate peasants who made up the bulk of the camp populations. After all, countries like Syria and Lebanon maintained, good land was scarce and their own peasants needed all they could get.

As a result, the camps of cluttered huts and tents remained year after year, decade after decade. As of mid-1981, UNRWA listed almost 1,900,000 people on its registration rolls. This astonishingly high figure partly reflected a high birthrate among the refugees; it also reflected the inability of UNRWA to clear the rolls of fraudulent entries (dead people, nonexistent people, non-refugees) for fear of causing riots among the volatile camp people. Through June 1981, the United States had provided more than $933 million, nearly half the $2 billion spent by UNRWA.

The attitude of the refugees has not helped either. Restless and unhappy in the crowded, sometimes filthy

[60]

camps, most of them still refused to take the training offered by the UN that would have enabled them to leave the camps and find employment in the Arab world. This, they argued, would amount to a renunciation of their right to return to Palestine—to lands now part of Israel. Many young Palestinians have lived their entire lives in the camps, hearing their elders spin stories about their homes in Palestine and how the Israelis took them away. Little wonder that the PLO found the refugee camps such fruitful ground for recruitment.

ISRAEL'S NEW ARABS

Until the Six-Day War of 1967, Israel, as pointed out in the previous chapter, had little trouble with its relatively small Palestinian population. But the Palestinian Arabs living in territories occupied during the war—the West Bank, the Gaza Strip, and the Old City of Jerusalem—now presented Israel with a major problem. For there were 700,000 Arabs on the West Bank and 300,000 in the Gaza Strip. Added to the 400,000 living in Israel itself, almost a million and a half Palestinian Arabs, most of them hostile, were being ruled by roughly twice that many Jews.

Culturally, the two groups were poles apart, and few on either side made much attempt to understand the other. Most of the Arabs under Israeli rule were unlearned and unsophisticated; many were Bedouins who had spent their lives moving with their sheep from one water hole to the next. The vast majority retained traditional Arab views. They regarded physical labor as degrading, something left to subject races or slaves. Most of these Arabs could not operate the simplest piece of equipment; winding a clock, to those few interested in knowing the time, was an adventure. Their attitude toward women was simple: women were inferior; their place was in the home, washing the clothes, stirring the lentils, and tending the swarms of children.

The Israelis were a sharp and irritating contrast. Blunt and aggressive, most of them shared a "work ethic" that made them doers and achievers. And, to the disgust of the Arabs, Israeli women acted as if they were the equals of men, even to the point of serving in the army! Even more horrifying, many Israeli women displayed their bodies by wearing shorts in public.

Israeli policies also created problems, particularly on the West Bank. Contrary to international law prohibiting the creation of permanent settlements on conquered territory, successive Israeli governments permitted hundreds of settlements to be established, often by young religious Jews. These settlers believed that the land was theirs by right, since the West Bank—when it was known as Judea and Samaria—was inhabited by Jews in ancient times. To the Arabs this growing number of settlements was nothing more or less than "creeping annexation" by Israel of the West Bank of the Jordan. The United Nations passed resolution after resolution condemning the settlements; the United States, on many occasions, called on Israel to halt the settlements. But year after year, the settlements multiplied, and after Menachem Begin, the former Irgun leader, became prime minister in 1977, the program was accelerated.

After the shock of the Six-Day War wore off, the Arabs of the West Bank became increasingly defiant of the Israeli authorities. In protest against particular Israeli policies, shopkeepers closed their shops, workers went on strike, and students demonstrated in the streets. Palestinian children, sometimes for the benefit of TV cameras, hurled rocks at tense Israeli soldiers. All too often, the Israelis responded harshly, beating up the rock throwers or even burning down the homes of suspected troublemakers. The Israelis imprisoned young people for months without charges, usually because they suspected them of sympathizing with the guerrillas. They forcibly removed elected local mayors from office when those Arab officials spoke out against Israeli policies. Needless

[62]

to say, the Israeli policies on the West Bank deepened Palestinian hatred for the occupiers and created a steady stream of recruits for the guerrillas.

THE PALESTINE LIBERATION ORGANIZATION

Another result of the Six-Day War was the spectacular rise of the Palestine Liberation Organization. Under its original leader, Ahmed Shukairy, the PLO had not made much of an impact. In the early 1960s, anti-Israel guerrilla operations were carried out by a number of separate groups, some of them numbering no more than a few dozen, that had no official ties to the PLO. Yasir Arafat's al-Fatah, backed by the Syrians at the time, was the most numerous and successful of the guerrilla groups.

Shortly after the Six-Day War, representatives of these Palestinian guerrilla groups met in Damascus, Syria, to discuss joint operations. But the political and tactical views of the various leaders were too disparate for any consensus to emerge. Fatah resumed its operations while three of the smaller groups united to form the Popular Front for the Liberation of Palestine (PFLP). Its leader was George Habash, a medical doctor, a Marxist intellectual, and a man who came to believe that any action that harmed Israel—skyjacking, sabotage, terrorism—was justified. If innocent civilians were harmed, well, that was just too bad. At that time, Arafat's al-Fatah was less radical in its politics and preferred to concentrate on military objectives rather than spectacular terrorist stunts.

In 1968, Arafat moved his main operational base to Jordan, where King Hussein at first made no objections to the presence of the guerrillas. After numerous forays by the Fatah commandos against military targets on the West Bank, the Israelis struck back by sending tanks and troops into Jordan to attack the guerrilla bases. Near the town of Karameh, Jordanian troops joined with the fedayeen (from the Arabic word for "sacrificers") to beat back the Israelis, killing twenty-six of them and wounding another seventy. It was a minor triumph, but because it was the first Arab triumph since the Six-Day War, the incident greatly heightened Arafat's prestige in the Arab world. In Cairo in 1969, leaders of the various Palestinian guerrilla groups prevailed on the Arab League to oust the ineffective Shukairy as head of the PLO and install Arafat as its leader. He promptly converted the PLO into an umbrella organization that included a number of guerrilla groups of differing political shadings: the leaders of each group became members of the PLO's executive body, the Palestine National Committee (PNC).

THE COVENANT

The basic document that has guided all the groups that form the PLO is the Palestinian Covenant. First drafted by Shukairy, it was accepted by Arafat and the other guerrilla leaders when they assumed leadership in 1969. The document is quite explicit in its repudiation of Israel's right to exist. Says the Covenant: "The establishment of Israel is fundamentally null and void." The general message of the Covenant is that Palestine is the homeland of the Palestinian Arabs, a homeland which must not be separated from the Arab world. The whole of Palestine must be returned to the Arab Palestinians. To abolish Israel would not only be legal, it would benefit the Arabs, the Palestinians, and humanity in general.

This does not mean that every guerrilla in the PLO accepts every word of the Covenant or interprets it in the same way. It cannot be emphasized sufficiently that the PLO is not a monolithic group. It is composed of different guerrilla groups which often differ on policy and tactics. But Arafat, as the head of the most important group, al-Fatah, has been the number-one man since 1969; as of mid-1982, he was still the top leader.

In addition to Fatah, a number of other guerrilla

[64]

groups have been in and out of the PLO tent. Among them are the following:

The Popular Front for the Liberation of Palestine (PFLP). Led by the Marxist Dr. George Habash, who in the late 1970s shifted his allegiance away from Moscow and toward Peking, the PFLP has close ties with radical terrorist groups in Asia. Using Japanese terrorists as his tools, Habash was behind the bloody massacre of twenty-seven people—most of them non-Jewish tourists—at Israel's Lod airport in 1972.

The Popular Democratic Front for the Liberation of Palestine (PDFLP). Headed by Nayef Hawatmeh, a Christian Bedouin, this group split away from Habash's organization on the grounds that Habash was not sufficiently leftist. The goriest exploit of this pro-Soviet group was the killing of more than twenty school children and adults, and the wounding of seventy more, in their seizure of a schoolhouse at Maalot, Israel, in May 1974.

The Popular Front for the Liberation of Palestine–General Command. Another offshoot of Habash's organization, this group is led by a former Syrian army captain and demolition expert named Ahmed Jebreel. The General Command claimed responsibility for an explosion aboard an Israeli El Al airliner over Switzerland in February 1972; thirty-eight passengers and nine crew members died.

As Saiqa ("Thunderbolt"). Closely tied to the Syrian army, it is more involved in intra-Arab politics than in outright guerrilla operations.

The Arab Liberation Front. This group is a creation of Iraq; its chief purpose seems to be keeping an eye on the other groups.

[65]

The Arab National Youth Organization for the Liberation of Palestine (ANYOLP). Backed by Libya's belligerent strongman Muammar Qaddafi, this group specialized in international skyjacking in the 1970s. When Arafat, seeking a more respectable image abroad, rejected the practice of skyjacking, ANYOLP defied him and said it would continue to seize aircraft. Arafat vowed to squelch the group, so its current status is unknown.

Although some of these groups considered Arafat and al-Fatah as moderate, or "gradualist," Fatah itself was no stranger to terrorism. The Black September contingent, most of whose members are from Fatah, killed Jordanian King Hussein's right-hand man Wasfi Tal in the streets of Cairo in November 1971. The fanatical group massacred eleven Israeli Olympic athletes in Munich in September 1972. It slaughtered two American diplomats and one Belgian in the Sudanese capital of Khartoum in March of 1973.

SHOWDOWN
IN JORDAN
As chief of the PLO, Arafat became a magnet for young Palestinians eager to take up arms against Israel. And so, during 1969 and early 1970, Arafat's ranks in Jordan swelled until he commanded 10,000 armed men. The PLO also had an unknown number of sympathizers among Palestinians living in Jordan.

By now, King Hussein began to grow nervous at the growing PLO presence in his land. Arafat and the PLO guerrillas swaggered around the Jordanian capital of Amman, refusing to acknowledge the authority of the Jordanian police or army. The guerrillas ran their own camps and tried to operate as a "state within a state." Seeing Jordan's sovereignty flouted by the Palestinians, Hussein became enraged. His relations with the PLO

[66]

came to a flash point in September 1970, when the guerrillas hijacked three planes in international skies and brought two of them to a remote Jordanian airstrip, where they held the passengers hostage for days before releasing them unharmed.

That escapade was enough for the king, who ordered a crackdown on the guerrillas. Hussein's tough Bedouin army units—which despised the Palestinians as trouble-making outsiders—were delighted to get the orders.

In a battle lasting four days, they killed thousands of the guerrillas and sent the rest fleeing for their lives into Syria. A few held out for months in the Jordanian forests, but they eventually were wiped out by the Jordanian army. For the PLO, this was indeed a black September. The terrorist unit of Fatah mentioned earlier—Black September—took its name from the bloody events in Jordan.

From September 1970, until into the early 1980s, the main body of the PLO was based in Syria and, in even greater strength, in Lebanon. There, a weak government was unable to control the Palestinian guerrillas, who treated Lebanese authorities with contempt and carried out operations against the Israelis without regard for the punishment it might bring to the Lebanese.

THE OCTOBER WAR
AND ITS AFTERMATH

If their ejection from Jordan was a stiff blow to the PLO, the October War of 1973 gave a lift to their spirits—at least at the beginning. In the early days of that war—called the Yom Kippur War by the Israelis because Egypt and Syria launched it on the Jewish holy day—the Arab armies made substantial gains against the Israelis. A clear-cut victory by Egypt and Syria would have given the PLO, and Palestinians in general, hope that they might return to their homes.

[67]

These hopes were dashed when the Israelis counter-attacked, pushing back the Syrians and threatening to cut off large numbers of Egyptian troops. When the war was over, the Israelis, though initially caught off guard, once again had demonstrated their military superiority. But the Egyptians and Syrians had showed themselves capable of waging modern warfare; in their early victories, they destroyed the image of Israeli invincibility. The Israelis themselves were badly shaken; their sense of security—and of superiority—was temporarily shattered.

The Palestinians, including the PLO, viewed the final outcome of the October War with mixed emotions. On the plus side was the partial success of Arab arms. Another plus from the Palestinian point of view was the willingness of the Arab states to stand behind their cause with more than just rhetoric. In support of the Arab, and Palestinian cause, the Organization of Petroleum Exporting Countries (OPEC), made up chiefly of Arab countries, slapped an embargo on oil shipments to the United States, Israel's chief supporter. OPEC also cut oil shipments to western Europe, as a warning to countries considered too friendly to Israel. This was the first use of the "oil-weapon." In unleashing it, the Arabs suddenly compelled the world at large to pay more attention to Arab views, including those on Palestine.

The October War also produced some definite minuses for the PLO. Chief among these was the emergence of the United States as the key diplomatic factor in the Middle East. President Anwar Sadat of Egypt, whose troops had performed extremely well during the October War, desperately wanted a long-term peace with Israel so that his country could channel its energies into improving the life of its people. And Sadat was convinced that only the United States had the power and influence to make the Israelis bargain seriously.

As the Palestinians looked on suspiciously, Sadat

[68]

and U.S. Secretary of State Henry Kissinger formed a close working relationship. In early 1974, the American began to shuttle between Jerusalem and various Arab capitals in an effort to "disengage" Israeli troops from Egyptian and Syrian troops. Despite the objections by Israeli and Arab hardliners, including most of the PLO, Kissinger managed to work out a series of agreements that disengaged the opposing forces. The Israelis pulled back from all territory taken from the Syrians in 1973 as well as a sliver of Syrian territory taken in 1967. The Israelis also withdrew to about 20 miles (32 km) east of the Suez Canal, allowing Egypt to reopen the international waterway.

It was a brilliant piece of diplomacy by Kissinger, one that established the United States as the only outside power that could produce concrete results in the region. Diplomatic relations between Washington and Cairo and Washington and Damascus, severed during the 1967 fighting because of American support for Israel, were resumed. Such was the improvement of the American image in the Middle East that President Richard Nixon made a tour of the region in 1974 and was cordially, if not triumphantly, received. In Egypt, Nixon's reception was enthusiastic as huge crowds lined the streets of Cairo, waving American flags.

This was not good news for the PLO. Most Arabs, and particularly the Palestinians, were convinced that the United States was too deeply committed to Israel to be evenhanded. Moreover, many in the PLO ranks were Marxists and thus ideologically hostile to the United States, regarded as the bastion of capitalism. On a more practical level, most of the fedayeen were dependent on the Russians for arms, and the Soviets and their friends in the ranks of the PLO certainly looked askance at any expanding role for the United States in the region.

Anwar Sadat's enhanced reputation in the Arab world as a result of the October War was also far from welcome to the PLO. Even before the war, the Egyptian president had offered to sign a peace treaty with Israel, fully recognizing the Jewish state in exchange for an Israeli withdrawal from territories it seized in 1967. To the PLO at that time, recognition of Israel was tantamount to betraying the cause of the Palestinian Arabs. And so, in the aftermath of the October War, the PLO kept a close and wary watch on President Sadat.

A SLIGHTLY NEW
IMAGE FOR THE PLO.

After the October War of 1973, the PLO assessed the new situation. In the executive body of the PLO, the Palestine National Council, the debate was heated. Arafat and his supporters, now considered "moderates" by the other guerrilla groups, argued that Israel, so staunchly backed by the United States, was an unpalatable reality that had to be accepted. The stale rhetoric about driving Israel into the sea, they maintained, had to be abandoned.

Moreover, Arafat and his "moderates" argued for a scaling-down of Palestinian objectives. Since there was little chance of regaining all of Palestine, why not accept a small state encompassing the West Bank and the Gaza Strip? Why not accept a ministate now and then see what the future brings?

Other important PLO leaders, including Habash, refused to give up, even as a matter of temporary tactics, their grand design of replacing Israel with a democratic, secular state covering the whole of what was Palestine before the 1948 partition. They continued to insist, in line with the Palestinian Covenant, that Israel would have to be dismantled. It must be remembered that some of these radicals, like Habash, were dedicated Marxists whose professions of democracy were open to question.

On the world scene, the year 1974 proved a banner one for both Arafat and the PLO. In October, Arab lead-

[70]

ers gathered at a summit meeting in Rabat, Morocco, and unanimously designated the PLO as the sole legitimate representative of the Palestinian people. This meant that Arab governments of every political stripe, from Marxist revolutionary governments such as Algeria and Yemen to the ultraconservative kingdoms of Saudi Arabia and Morocco, accepted the PLO as the rightful voice of the Palestinians. The Arab summit leaders also affirmed the right of the Palestinians to establish an independent nation under the PLO in any territory they "liberated" from the Israelis. In effect, this was an endorsement of Arafat's acceptance of the concept of a Palestinian ministate on the West Bank and in the Gaza Strip.

Additional prestige was bestowed on Arafat by the United Nations, and the reasons for this were not too difficult to divine. By 1974, the UN had become dominated by Third World countries—from Asia, Africa, and Latin America. First of all, many of these young countries had just gained their independence as the result of revolutionary struggle, and in a sense they identified with the Palestinians in their own fight for a national homeland. Second, many of the Third World countries were dominated by Marxists, who saw Israel as an outpost of "western imperialism" in the Middle East. Third, there was the question of oil. Most of the Third World countries were totally dependent on the Arab states for petroleum, and they hoped to win price concessions from the Arabs in exchange for taking a pro-Palestinian position at the United Nations.

Thus, from both the practical and ideological points of view, most of the Third World had come to favor the PLO. Not surprisingly, the Arab countries, plus the Soviet Union and its eastern European bloc, solidly supported the Palestinians. Under the circumstances, it was hardly astonishing that a majority at the United Nations, over strong U.S. and Israeli objections, invited

[71]

the PLO to participate in deliberations on the Palestinian issue.

In November 1974, Yasir Arafat received a near triumphant reception at the United Nations in New York. While the U.S. delegation fumed, while the Israelis fretted, and while the western Europeans tuttutted, Arafat was given all the honors usually reserved for a head of state. He was greeted at the UN by Secretary General Kurt Waldheim; he was given a hall at the UN to hold a reception for thousands; most importantly, he was allowed to address the General Assembly.

With a pistol on his hip, Arafat told the Assembly that he had come bearing "an olive branch and a freedom fighter's gun." But his speech contained little of the olive branch. Arafat warned the Israelis that his fedayeen would continue their struggle until victory; there was no hint of the conciliatory tone that he himself had taken in the debate within the PLO. Privately, Palestinians in New York explained that Arafat could not publicly express his own moderate views for fear of attack by extremists within the badly divided PLO. Despite Arafat's militant tone, the General Assembly voted soon thereafter to grant the PLO observer status at the United Nations. The guerrilla organization—critics called it a terrorist organization—was thereby given the same standing at the United Nations as North Korea, South Korea, and the Vatican.

Beyond any question, these events greatly enhanced the PLO's image in the world at large. Many non-Arab countries had come to regard the PLO as the sole legitimate voice of the Palestinian people, and some even extended full diplomatic recognition to the guerrilla organization. The vast majority of the Palestinian Arabs—whether they lived in Israel, the occupied territories, or the Palestinian Diaspora—accepted the PLO as spokesmen and fighters for their cause. In a few years, Yasir Arafat had created a force that the world—and the state of Israel—had to reckon with.

9
New Directions

Pleased with his newly acquired international respectability, Arafat modified his tactics, confining guerrilla attacks to Israeli territory and banning attacks in foreign countries or in the international skies. The PLO leader even began to arrest guerrillas who openly opposed this "moderate" policy and confine them in Lebanese hideouts. Still, radical elements within the PLO—backed by Libya and Iraq—defied Arafat and continued to carry out acts of international terrorism. Some of them were spectacular—and bloody.

TERROR AND COUNTERTERROR
In January 1975, two teams of terrorists from Jebreel's General Command tried to blow up two Israeli jetliners at Orly Airport in Paris. The terrorists fired off a number of rockets, which missed the aircraft but wounded eighteen people. They then seized ten hostages at the airport and released them only after a French plane flew them to Iraq. Jebreel was later interviewed on French television and declared that he would continue "suicide operations to disrupt a political settlement" he claimed was planned by Arafat.

Again defying Arafat, in mid-1975 the General

[73]

Command refused to release an American officer, Colonel Ernest Morgan, who had been kidnapped in Beirut by a smaller terrorist group and turned over to the Command. Jebreel rejected Arafat's demand that Morgan be freed. Only after the Syrian government sided with Arafat did Jebreel release the American.

Dr. Habash's PFLP also rejected Arafat's guidelines confining terrorist actions to Israel. In a spectacular incident in December 1975, six gun-wielding men invaded the Vienna headquarters of the Organization of Petroleum Exporting Countries (OPEC). They killed two of its Arab staff members and an Austrian policeman; then they captured eighty men and women, including the oil ministers of ten different countries. The gunmen read a statement to the press denouncing Arafat for his "gradualism," Egyptian President Sadat for negotiating with Israel through the United States, and OPEC for selling oil to the West. Threatening to kill their captives, the terrorists demanded and got an Austrian jetliner to fly to Algeria, then Libya, then back to Algeria. There they were finally talked into releasing their hostages in exchange for safe conduct out of the country to Libya. These terrorists, three Arabs and three westerners, labeled themselves the "Arab Armed Struggle Organization," a splinter group with close links to Habash's PFLP.

Meanwhile, Fatah and other PLO groups occupied themselves with raids on settlements in northern Israel or with planting bombs in crowded Israeli marketplaces. Grimly, the Israelis tightened their security measures and evolved a tough-minded policy toward terrorists. One part of Israel's policy was a steadfast refusal to trade off captured fedayeen for hostages; another part was a punishing campaign of counterterror. Israeli aircraft and ships attacked the Lebanese capital of Beirut and other Lebanese cities; Israeli commandos stormed ashore, capturing and killing known guerrilla leaders. In one dramatic operation, Israeli commandos landed on

[74]

the beaches of Beirut and followed intelligence agents to the homes and offices of guerrilla leaders. The Israelis smashed up the offices of Fatah and other groups; in the very heart of Beirut they forced their way into apartments and shot dead three known Fatah leaders. Then the Israelis climbed aboard their ships with bags of captured documents, which later helped them to identify and arrest PLO agents among the Arab population of Israel.

The most famous counterterrorist stroke by the Israelis came in mid-1976, after three men and a woman—who identified themselves as part of Habash's PFLP—hijacked a huge Air France plane en route from Tel Aviv to Paris. They forced the pilot to fly to Uganda, where the hijackers were greeted as friends and heroes by dictator Idi Amin. His troops were actually used to guard the hostages. The hijackers released over a hundred of the passengers, but they kept more than one hundred Jewish passengers under threat of execution. The terrorists demanded the release of fifty-three guerrillas from prisons in Israel, Kenya, and Europe.

The Israeli government seemed prepared to negotiate, but secretly it organized a rescue mission. On July 3, Israeli aircraft loaded with elite troops flew the 2,600 miles (4,200 km) to Uganda, swooped down on the airport at Entebbe, killed seven out of eight terrorists (the four hijackers had been joined by accomplices in Uganda), and twenty Ugandan soldiers. The commandos rescued the entire crew and 103 passengers and flew them out to Israel. Three hostages and one Israeli officer died in the raid; one elderly female passenger who was in the local hospital when the raid took place was later murdered by angry Ugandan soldiers. It was the most daring and successful antiterrorist mission on record.

ENTER THE SYRIANS

Another blow to the Palestinian guerrillas was dealt by the Syrian army. In 1975, Lebanon had erupted into civil

[75]

war, with heavy fighting taking place in many parts of the country. On one side were Muslim leftists backed by elements of the PLO; on the other were right-wing Christians. By early 1976, the bloodshed had reached such proportions (the number of dead was conservatively estimated at twenty thousand) that leaders of the Arab League came to the conclusion that outside intervention was necessary. The League asked Syria to send a peace-keeping force into Lebanon to keep the war-torn country from complete disintegration. The Syrians were willing, and in June 1976, Syrian tanks and troops crossed into Lebanon.

Hafez Assad, the Syrian president, wished to bring the fighting among the various Lebanese factions to a halt at once. For one thing, his influence and prestige in the Arab world was at stake; for another, if the turbulence continued, the Israelis might be tempted to move into Lebanon and establish a sphere of influence. But the guerrillas wanted the chaos to continue. Major elements in the PLO clearly wanted to see Lebanon remain divided and feeble, so they could continue operations against Israel without trouble from the Lebanese.

As the Syrian army rolled close to Beirut, some of the extremist elements in the PLO, including Habash's PFLP, turned their arms against them. The Syrian troops fired back and took a heavy toll of fedayeen. In Tel Aviv, in May of 1976, Israeli Prime Minister Yitzhak Rabin was able to remark: "In Lebanon, Syrian forces or forces under Syrian command (As Saiqa guerrillas) have killed more guerrillas in that last week than Israel has killed in the last two years." The Syrians quickly established themselves as a stabilizing force in Lebanon, keeping Muslims and Christians from each other's throats and keeping Palestinian guerrilla operations against Israel to a minimum. So as not to alarm the Israelis, the Syrian troops stayed in north Lebanon, away from the border with Israel.

[76]

KISSINGERIAN DIPLOMACY

The late 1970s was not a good time for the PLO on the diplomatic front, either. Arafat and Fatah, though not Marxist politically, had moved closer to the Soviet Union for very practical reasons. They needed Russian arms and Russian political support in such bodies as the United Nations. The Soviet Union, for its part, backed Arafat in the endless intrigues and struggles within the PLO, since Moscow regarded the bearded guerrilla leader as more responsible, and perhaps more manageable, than ardent leftists like Dr. Habash.

To the distress of Arafat and his Russian supporters, the United States—in the person of Secretary of State Henry Kissinger—continued to play a vigorous diplomatic role in the Middle East. Arafat feared that Kissinger would negotiate a deal between Egypt and Israel that would mean the end of Egyptian participation in wars for the sake of an Arab Palestine. The Russians squirmed at being replaced by the United States as the chief influence on Egypt, the most important country in the Arab world.

In September 1975, after another series of arduous shuttles between Cairo and Tel Aviv, Kissinger was able to negotiate a second disengagement agreement between Israeli and Egyptian forces in the Sinai. In addition to providing for a further Israeli withdrawal from the Suez Canal area, the document contained other, even more significant provisions: a new buffer zone between Egyptian and Israeli forces controlled by a United Nations peace-keeping force; American monitoring of the agreement by aerial reconnaissance and electronic surveillance stations; the transit of nonmilitary Israeli ships through the Suez Canal; and—of greatest importance— a mutual commitment to use only peaceful means to resolve the Arab-Israeli dispute over Palestine.

This last proviso, which removed the Egyptians as a factor in any future military confrontation with Israel, enraged many Arabs, and particularly the Palestinians, for it clearly meant that Egypt—the Arab world's most powerful military force—had no intention of spilling any more blood for the Palestinian cause. Egypt's president Anwar Sadat, nevertheless, continued to discuss the Palestinian problem in his pursuit of peace with Israel.

SADAT'S VISION

When Jimmy Carter became president of the United States in January 1977, Sadat—convinced more than ever that Washington was the key to a lasting peace in the Middle East—embarked on a campaign to establish close ties with the new president. He visited Washington in April, and at that time emphasized to Carter that the heart of the problem of peace in the Middle East was the Palestinian question.

Sadat recalls in his memoirs that he told President Carter that all other Arab-Israeli problems are "symptoms of a central malaise which is summed up in the Palestinian problem." The Egyptian president also made it clear to Carter that Egypt, for one, now favored a genuine state of peace with Israel, including full diplomatic recognition and any guarantees Israel wanted about secure borders. In exchange, Sadat asked that Israel withdraw from the Arab lands it seized in the 1967 war and make a serious effort to come to grips with the Palestinian question. Specifically, Sadat proposed the establishment of a Palestinian state on the West Bank of the Jordan and the Gaza Strip.

After his trip to Washington, Sadat embarked on a reappraisal of what could be done to achieve peace with Israel—and achieve a Palestinian state. The result was Sadat's astounding offer to go to Jerusalem, the capital of Israel, on a mission of peace. Israeli Prime Minister Menachem Begin at first did not know what to make of the offer, but he extended an invitation within a matter of days. Sadat accepted it, and—over the objections of some of his advisers—flew to Jerusalem.

[78]

It was a remarkable gesture and a remarkable event. Sadat prayed in Al Aqsa Mosque in Jerusalem, one of the holiest Muslim shrines, and then delivered an historic address to the Israeli parliament. Before the hushed assemblage, he told the Israeli nation that, after thirty years on a wartime footing, Egypt accepted the right of the Jewish state to exist as a sovereign country within secure borders. Sadat also stated that he understood Israel's need for security and for guarantees by international bodies of that security. But the Egyptian president added bluntly that Israel would have to pay a price: withdrawal to the borders existing before the 1967 war and a recognition of the right of the Palestinians to their own state on the West Bank and in the Gaza Strip.

Sadat had broken the ice. From his subsequent meetings at Camp David, Maryland, with Prime Minister Begin and President Carter came the framework for the historic peace treaty between Israel and Egypt, which was signed in Washington in March, 1979. With the treaty Israel agreed to withdraw from the entire Sinai peninsula; Egypt agreed to establish full and friendly diplomatic relations with Israel. Both agreed to work toward an ill-defined full autonomy for the Palestinians on the West Bank and in Gaza.

The pact put an end to three decades of Egyptian-Israeli confrontation, but many Arabs and Palestinians were left to ponder how the Egyptian commitment to peace would affect their cause.

10

Today and Tomorrow

When Anwar Sadat signed the peace treaty with Israel, many people predicted that the Egyptian leader had also signed his own death warrant. For though his imaginative diplomacy and personal courage were applauded in the West and in other parts of the world, many Arabs felt that he had betrayed the cause of the Palestinian Arabs by making peace with Israel. Yasir Arafat stated openly that Sadat had sold out the Palestinian cause. One of his top associates was quoted as saying that "Sadat has given away Palestine. No wonder the Israelis love him." Habash and other Palestinian extremists called for Sadat's assassination.

Sadat was assassinated on October 6, 1981, as he sat on a reviewing stand for a military parade in Cairo. He was killed by Muslim fundamentalists, who could not forgive him for his relatively liberal, pro-Western inclinations. But they also made it plain that they murdered him for making peace with Israel. Fundamentalist Muslims allied to the killers termed Sadat's peace with Israel as "evil" and called for a *jihad*, or "holy war," against Israel. "Believers do not take the Jews and Christians as friends," read the leaflets handed out in the streets of Cairo by turbaned zealots.

[80]

Sadat's murder was greeted with jubilation among the extremist elements in the PLO camp. In Beirut, Palestinian guerrillas paraded through the streets brandishing posters of Sadat with an X-mark over his face. PLO officials called Sadat's slaying an "execution" rather than an assassination. This was a reminder of the Palestinian view that Sadat had met his just punishment for making peace with Israel before resolving the Palestinian issue. PLO security chief Salah Khalaf boasted that the PLO would "shake the hand of him who pulled the trigger." Palestinian mayors on the Israeli-occupied West Bank of the Jordan did not mourn Sadat either. "Sadat's death was no loss," said Bassam al Shakaa, mayor of Nablus. "We hope that the Egyptians will now return to the trenches of the nationalist Arabs and fight for Palestinian rights."

AFTER CAMP DAVID

For signing the peace treaty with Israel, Egypt had been ostracized in parts of the Arab world. Many Arab countries cut political and economic ties with Egypt. Privately, some of these countries—such as Saudi Arabia and the wealthy Persian Gulf states—believed that Sadat was on the right track. But at that time, given the state of anti-Israel opinion in their countries, their leaders were unable to say so publicly. These other Arab states simply did not believe that the time had come to make peace with Israel.

In spite of Arab opposition, Israel and Egypt complied with the provisions of the peace treaty. The two countries established full diplomatic relations, exchanging ambassadors and opening their borders to each other's tourists and businessmen, and the Begin government carried out its pledge to withdraw from the Sinai peninsula.

Not surprisingly, however, the Camp David peace process became snagged on the issue of the Palestinians. Sadat and Begin had agreed that one of the main com-

[81]

ponents of peace between Israel and the Arabs would have to be negotiations toward "full" Palestinian autonomy on the West Bank and in the Gaza Strip. In the early 1980s, those talks made little progress, despite sporadic efforts by Washington to spur the Israelis and Egyptians into action.

The chief obstacle was the attitude of the Israeli government of Menachem Begin, a conservative coalition that included several religious parties and had no intention of allowing the Palestinian Arabs on the West Bank and in Gaza to exercise a substantial degree of autonomy. First, they thought that Arabs with any degree of autonomy on the West Bank would be pro-PLO and a serious security threat to Israel. Second, the Begin government considered the West Bank—Judea and Samaria, as he and the religious Jews called it—to be Jewish (i.e., Israeli) territory. As Begin gave lip service to the Camp David agreement providing for "full autonomy" for the Palestinian Arabs on the West Bank and in Gaza, his government continually subverted that concept by encouraging new Jewish settlements in these occupied territories.

In 1982, most analysts believed that Israel—unless restrained by the United States—eventually would attempt to annex the West Bank and Gaza. Precedent had been established. In 1980, Israel annexed the Old City of Jerusalem; in 1981, it annexed the Golan Heights of Syria. Both had been taken in the 1967 Six-Day War. It was becoming clear that Israel was determined to hang on to its conquests, and that the return of the Sinai to Egypt was a unique case.

ARAB DISUNITY

The nations of the Arab world were far from united in their approach to the Palestine issue. The so-called rejectionist countries—Syria, Iraq, Libya, and Yemen—opposed any sort of compromise with Israel. Iran, Muslim but non-Arab, also preached the hard anti-Israeli line under the leadership of the Ayatollah Khomeini and his mullahs. But these rejectionists are not a solid, like-minded bloc. On issues other than Israel they had deep disagreements, often passionate, sometimes violent.

By the early 1980s, the rest of the Arab countries, often labeled "moderates," had given up hope of erasing Israel from the map. All publicly had endorsed U.N. Resolution 242, which implicitly recognized Israel. This group included Saudi Arabia, Jordan, the oil-rich sheikhdoms of the Persian Gulf, Morocco and Tunisia, the Sudan and Somalia. Egypt, of course, had taken the lead. After Sadat's death, his peacemaking efforts with Israel came to seem not quite so disgraceful to the moderates, who cautiously began to hold out the hand of friendship to his successor, Hosni Mubarak. Though these moderates differed among themselves in degree, basically they would recognize Israel's right to exist behind secure borders in exchange for an Israeli withdrawal from the Arab lands it seized in 1967. They favored the establishment of a Palestinian ministate on the West Bank and in the Gaza Strip.

THE CRUX OF THE MATTER

The Palestinian people remained the crux of the conflict between Israel and the Arabs. Estimates of the total number of Palestinian Arabs in 1982, both refugees and nonrefugees, ranged from 3.6 million to 4.4 million. Estimates based on U.S. State Department figures show that of this total, more than 550,000 lived as citizens of Israel; many more lived in the occupied territories—nearly 100,000 in the Arab section of Jerusalem, over 450,000 in the Gaza district, and 833,000 on the West Bank. Of the Palestinians living abroad, more than a million lived in Jordan, approximately 360,000 in Lebanon, and 225,000 in Syria. Most of the rest were concentrated in the Persian Gulf area, with approximately 300,000 in Kuwait, 137,000 in Saudi Arabia, and another 83,000 in Iraq, the United Arab Emirates, Bahrein, and Qatar. An

[83]

estimated 46,000 Palestinians were in Egypt, and 23,000 more lived in Libya. Another 250,000 Palestinians were scattered through Europe and America.

By and large, these Palestinians were not resigned to remaining stateless people. Many of them did not necessarily want to leave their present homes and move back to the ancestral land. But almost all strongly favored a geographical homeland as a mark of national identity. A large percentage of the Palestinians still living in the UN-sponsored refugee camps expressed the desire, if it were possible, to return to Palestine.

In the early 1980s, the Arab population on the West Bank and in Gaza grew increasingly restive. Violent clashes between Israeli troops and rock-throwing young Arabs were frequent. The Israelis permitted the Arabs to elect their own mayors, but when the mayors turned out to sympathize with the PLO, the Israelis ousted them from office. The result was rioting, with the killing of Arab civilians by Israeli troops, and an even more intense hatred for the occupiers. The Israelis tried to set up an alternative Palestinian leadership to the pro-PLO mayors by establishing "village leagues" of Palestinians they believed were more cooperative. The leaders of these village leagues became so unpopular among the West Bank Palestinians that the Israelis had to provide them with bodyguards. Even during hard times for the PLO, the Palestinian Arabs of the West Bank remained loyal to Yasir Arafat and his diverse cohorts.

Within the PLO, serious divisions remained. Walking a tightrope between various factions in the organization, Arafat wavered considerably in his public utterances, first taking a hard line, then a seemingly flexible one. On one occasion, he sought to quiet Western fears that a Palestinian state run by the PLO would be Soviet-controlled, arguing that the new state would have to start "from ground zero" and would be too busy building that state to be a threat to anyone. Neither Israel, nor many

[84]

in the West, were convinced by that argument. To these doubters, it stood to reason that the Soviet Union, having supported the PLO so staunchly, would have considerable influence in an independent Palestinian state.

But in 1982, these arguments were strictly academic, for the likelihood of a Palestinian Arab state under the control of the PLO seemed increasingly remote. Having been evicted from Jordan, the PLO established another "state within a state" in Lebanon, where a succession of feeble governments were unable to control the guerrillas. From Lebanese territory the PLO launched many bloody raids on Israeli settlements; from the Lebanese capital of Beirut, Yasir Arafat and his associates directed a guerrilla campaign that struck at Israeli civilians and Israeli diplomats in foreign capitals. Over the years, Israel made a number of limited incursions into Lebanon to punish the guerrillas, but finally, in June of 1982, it mounted a full-scale invasion of Lebanon in an effort to destroy the PLO.

Sweeping up the Mediterranean coast and through the mountains to the east, Israeli armored forces, backed by stinging air strikes, quickly occupied a large part of Lebanon. The Israelis clashed briefly with Syrian troops, who had been in Lebanon since 1976 to enforce a truce among that unhappy country's numerous warring factions. But the chief Israeli target was the PLO. Israeli jets, gunboats, and artillery battered PLO strongholds in the cities of Sidon, Tyre, Beirut, and elsewhere. Thousands of PLO guerrillas were killed and many more wounded and taken captive.

When the Israelis besieged the beautiful Mediterranean city of Beirut, where the main body of PLO guerrillas was holed up, they bombed and shelled their targets relentlessly. Many civilians were killed in this onslaught. (This was not the fault of the Israelis alone: the PLO had chosen to place their bases in civilian neighborhoods.) Finally, under a plan worked out by U.S. Special Envoy Philip Habib, Arafat and his guerrillas agreed to leave Beirut for havens in Syria, Jordan, Egypt, Algeria, Tunisia, and other Arab countries.

At the start of the Israeli invasion, the stated objective was to drive the PLO out of Lebanese territory within 25 miles (40 km) of the northernmost Israeli border. The goal, supposedly, was to prevent the shelling of Israeli settlements. But as the invasion progressed, it became clear that Israel's objectives were far more elaborate. For one thing, the Israelis hoped to drive the Syrians out of Lebanon; for another, they seemed determined to kill or capture as many PLO guerrillas as possible and drive the rest of them out of the country. Finally, the Israelis apparently aimed to have a government established in Beirut that would be strong enough to keep the PLO out of the country.

While the Israeli invasion of Lebanon was successful as a military operation, it could not hope to solve the political problems of Palestine and the Palestinian Arabs. (This fact was dramatized in September, 1982, when hundreds of Palestinian civilians in Beirut refugee camps were massacred by groups of Lebanese Christians while the camps were under Israeli guard.) Nor could it destroy the PLO. One guerrilla leader likened the organization to a drop of mercury: strike it and it divides into numerous droplets moving in unpredictable directions. Its structure, leadership, and geographical base might change, but the organization itself would not easily be eradicated.

The question of Palestine has existed for thousands of years, and it is not likely to disappear in our time. The descendants of Abraham and the followers of Mohammed still contend for all or parts of the strip of territory known as the Holy Land. The opposing claims are not easy to judge. Both sides have historical and moral arguments to make. What does the future hold for Palestine? It would be foolish to predict. All that can be said is that the story has not yet ended.

[86]

For Further Reading

A vast amount of reading material on the Palestine Question is available. A brief selection of recommended books follows.

An excellent, lively history of the Jews and their relation to Palestine from the time of Abraham to the present is *Jews, God and History* by Max I. Dimont (New York: Simon and Schuster, 1962). Two other comprehensive, readable accounts of Jewish history are *Wanderings* by novelist Chaim Potok (New York: Knopf, 1975) and *A History of the Jews* by Solomon Grayzel (Philadelphia: Jewish Publication Society of America, 1947, 1968).

An interesting, scholarly book sympathetic to the Jewish position on Palestine is *Whose Land?* by James Parkes (New York: Taplinger, 1971). Another frankly pro-Zionist work is the briskly written *Israel: Land of the Jews* by Mina and Arthur Klein (Indianapolis: Bobbs-Merrill, 1972).

A classic study of the revival of Arab nationalism in the late nineteenth and early twentieth centuries is *The Arab Awakening* by George Antonius (New York: Putnam, 1946). For a crisply written introduction to Arab history and culture, as well as to the conflict between

[87]

Jews and Arabs over Palestine, a highly recommended book is *The Arabs: People and Power* prepared by the editors of the Encylopedia Britannica (New York: Bantam Books, 1978). Peter Mansfield's *The Arab World* (New York: Thomas Y. Crowell, 1976) is a well-written, pro-Palestinian book which traces the history of the Arabs from their early nomadic beginnings to the dispute with the Jews over Palestine. Another pro-Palestinian work, concentrating on the Arab-Israeli dispute over the Holy Land in the past few decades, is Fred J. Khouri's *The Arab-Israeli Dilemma* (Syracuse, NY: Syracuse University Press, 1968, 1976).

Of particular value for readers interested in the Arab-Jewish struggle in Palestine during the years of the British Mandate are *The Palestine Triangle* by Nicholas Bethell (New York: Putnam, 1979) and *Exile and Return* by Martin Gilbert (Philadelphia and New York: Lippincott, 1978). A very personal account of events leading up to Israeli independence is given in *The Revolt* by Menachem Begin, then the leader of the Irgun and now prime minister of Israel (New York: Nash, 1977).

A superb history of Nazi Germany and the tragedy that befell the Jews during that period is told in *The Rise and Fall of the Third Reich* by William L. Shirer (New York: Simon and Schuster, 1960).

An interesting examination of the Palestine Liberation Organization, as well as other revolutionary movements, is contained in Thomas Raynor's *Terrorism: Past, Present, Future* (New York: Franklin Watts, 1982).

Index